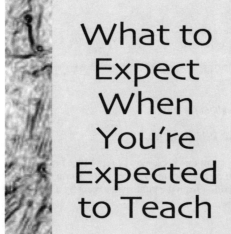

What to Expect When You're Expected to Teach

The Anxious Craft of Teaching Composition

Edited by
Anne Bramblett &
Alison Knoblauch

Introduction by Thomas Newkirk

Boynton/Cook Publishers
HEINEMANN
Portsmouth, NH

Boynton/Cook Publishers, Inc.
A subsidiary of Reed Elsevier Inc.
361 Hanover Street
Portsmouth, NH 03801–3912
www.boyntoncook.com

Offices and agents throughout the world

Library of Congress Cataloging-in-Publication Data
What to expect when you're expected to teach : the anxious craft of teaching composition / edited by Anne Bramblett and Alison Knoblauch ; introduction by Thomas Newkirk.
    p. cm.
Includes bibliographical references.
ISBN 0-86709-535-0 (alk. paper)
    1. English language—Rhetoric—Study and teaching. 2. Report writing—Study and teaching (Higher). 3. Teacher-student relationships. 4. Grading and marking (Students). I. Bramblett, Anne. II. Knoblauch, Alison.

PE1404 .W455 2002
808'.042'071–dc21   2002004412

Editor: Thomas Newkirk
Production services: Lisa Garboski, bookworks
Production coordination: Vicki Kasabian
Cover design: Joni Doherty
Typesetter: TechBooks, Inc.
Manufacturing: Steve Bernier

Printed in the United States of America on acid-free paper
06 05 04 03 02 DA 1 2 3 4 5

Contents

Silences in Our Teaching Stories: What Do We Leave Out and Why?

"As I read the literature on whole language/writing process classrooms, I wonder if we are not creating the role of 'super teacher,' one more ideal, without cracks, that creates a sense of inadequacy in all of us. Are there silences in the narratives we tell of our . . . classrooms? Are we telling everything? Do these consistently upbeat stories capture the emotional underlife of teaching? I think not."

"The ball is in my court. I've never taught this class before. I haven't had much opportunity to brainstorm with other instructors about it because everyone else is just as busy as I am, and they seem busier. I don't want to ask how to teach the class I self-assuredly said I would teach, and I don't want to be standing here while my new students all sense a Springer moment brewing."

"I launched into my first question . . . only to realize with horror that my plan had failed: their eyes were averted, their bodies slouched deep into their chairs. . . . Suddenly my classroom community became a hackneyed scene from a Sunday Western. It was me against them, staring as we fingered our guns. Who would the silence break first?"

threat of a GPA-devastating B+ was not at all far away. But then suddenly there I was, holding GPA devastators in the palm of my hand. There I was, sitting at the big desk with a grade book and no idea how to use it."

"Luke's conference is the only one that I remember clearly months later, though, because he directly, though no doubt unintentionally, challenged this authority that I was desperately trying to muster in my class. His resistance to the process of revision struck at my rather deep insecurities concerning my qualifications to teach the class. I couldn't offer him a satisfyingly concrete, empirical answer to his recurrent question, 'What's wrong with my paper?' "

" . . . I started my work at UNH viewing my class as a more or less homogenous front—all white, all middle- to upper-class, all fluent in English. Any relationship with a new student population must begin, I suppose, from such a reduced perception. But it was not far into the semester before I realized there was more complexity here than I knew what to do with."

"My high school English teacher, Mrs. Schermer, made a deal with me about writing. The deal was that I could write the way I wanted to half the time, but I had to write her way the other half of the time. . . . I knew what she wanted and I understood the 'deal,' but I continued to subvert and resist her assignments. . . . Now that I'm teaching college composition, it's time for payback. And Jeff is my payback."

"And (I ask in a hushed voice) can you teach someone to want to ask questions? I wonder (and feel blasphemous): is he teachable? Are there students who, because of their socialization, are not teachable? Or, is it my identity that is the problem?"

"I was intrigued by Jason's defiance, his insistence that he 'sucked' at writing, when, at least in my opinion, he did not. I decided he would be my success story. I would change his view of writing."

"In the weeks before I undertook teaching English 401, I'd been warned about problem students: boys. Big tall half-men who would physically intimidate me and sneer at my assignments. No one mentioned problem girls."

Preface

Welcome. Whether you're a brand new teacher, one who is pursuing a higher degree at a new institution, or it's your first time teaching college-age students, this book is designed for you.

This book was conceived after our first semester of teaching, after hours of talking and complaining in each other's offices, and over countless plate-sized pancakes at Joyce's Kitchen. We talked about the student we had recently told was failing who had wept, the student who was missing class because she was attempting to get legal custody of her little sister, our anger at the student who had been listening to tiny headphones during lecture. Why, at even eight in the morning, did all our discussions center around teaching problems and anxieties? Why did we feel so unprepared for these issues?

Sure, we had prepared for teaching. We had read books; we were both secondary education dropouts in college. Before and during our August orientation we were given instructions on how to construct a syllabus, the first five assignments, and were signed up for English 910 (Tom Newkirk's Teaching College Composition Practicum course) where we'd get a chance to discuss with our peers our developing pedagogies. We jotted down notes during orientation about paper assignments, reader responses, group workshops. We stole ideas like crazy. Although nervous and intimidated, we walked into our first semester of teaching thinking that, despite our anxieties, we knew what we were getting ourselves into. Really, we had no idea.

Frustrated with our lack of a semester vision, the unexpected issues that kept emerging in our classes, the problems of dealing with a persistently resistant student the entire semester, we jokingly decided that someone, anyone, should have told us about this. But wait, we realized, weren't we, the new teaching assistants, the perfect sages? The ones to enlighten future generations of teaching assistants? If only we were so confident in our teaching.

Our laughter followed us that same day into Tom Newkirk's office where we told him our book idea. We wanted to put together a collection of essays from teaching assistants and instructors, those who had been in the trenches, that would help prepare new teachers for those things that no one else tells you. Our ideas were vague; we laughed at our own audacity. But Tom took us seriously. And what you have before you is the final product.

What we've attempted to produce is not only a collection of first-semester stories, but a site for honesty. It's hard for new teachers to admit that they have no idea what they're doing sometimes. It's hard to admit that classes aren't always going swimmingly, that we're confused, that we feel like we're faking it, that we're pretty sure we've made a huge mistake. Even having these thoughts make us feel like failures, and we're too scared to admit our insecurities to anyone else for fear that they'll point us out as the frauds we so feel like. All we hear around us are stories of success, and these success stories get rewarded. People nod their heads, smile, and seem to relate to them. And then those stories build. We talk about what worked wonderfully, what was amazing, how fabulous all our students are. And all the while most of us are actually thinking, who *are* these people? Did I get *all* the silent students? Does *everyone* have perfect classes? NO! They don't! After weeks of success story after success story, we somehow discovered that none of us felt like successes most of the time. In fact, many of us felt like failures a lot of the time. And so we decided that *these* stories needed to be given voice. People needed to hear that everybody screws up, and that screwing up doesn't make you a bad teacher. It's absolutely, totally, and completely NORMAL.

We're not telling you how to teach; we're not offering simple solutions to complex problems. Instead, we let TAs, former TAs, and instructors write about their problems their first year, their stumbling blocks. Some views on teaching conflict with one another, but instead of making a homogenous book of essays, with one pedagogy in mind, we have a fusion of ideas, experiences, and personalities. We envision our reader as a companion to theoretical texts that focus on the development of pedagogy. *What to Expect When You're Expected to Teach* accompanies new teachers during their first semesters, from their first insecure moments to the final weeks of perspective and evaluation. We like to think of the collection as breaking the silence of failure and anxiety, to be able to take a step back and laugh at ourselves. It is a subtle reminder that we are perhaps at our best as teachers when we are uncomfortable and when our previously held convictions about teaching, students, and ourselves are continuously being complicated, challenged, and refined.

We hope that you find comfort in our stories. We're human; we make mistakes. You will, too. And that's fine—that's to be expected.

Acknowledgments

We would like to thank Dr. Thomas Newkirk who, instead of laughing us out of his office when we proposed this book, encouraged and guided us through the process. We would also like to thank all our contributors, and UNH's amazing English 401 and 501 teaching staff (particularly those of you on the third floor). Thank you to Kelly Myers and David Gruber for all your help.

Alison would also like to thank: my amazing friends Heidi Nitzsche and Branda Long; my dearest Tricia; Kelly (again), who simply can't go back to California; and my family, especially Jill, Jane, Bill, Jess, and Anne who remind me that I'm not the only cool one.

Anne would like to thank: my mom and sister, Lori—keep bragging about me. And thanks to y'all back home in Virginia; Melissa, in particular, thanks for all the visits and the support.

A Note to the Reader

Instructions

We envisioned this reader to be used in two different ways. You could, of course, read through the entire text, cover to cover. We have organized the essays into sections that made sense to us, and put readings in an order that seemed topic appropriate. Within each section, authors approach the topics in a variety of ways, which provides the reader with a broad spectrum of viewpoints, opinions, and experiences. For those of you who would rather use the "hunt and peck" method, we've included a brief excerpt from the essays in the table of contents to make the hunting easier. We invite you to poke around, or to read an appropriate essay anytime you feel bewildered, anxious, or angry.

Need Some Context?

Here's some helpful background information about the collection of essays and the University of New Hampshire Composition program:

Almost all the contributors to this collection of essays teach or have taught in the University of New Hampshire composition department. The graduate program at UNH requires a master's or Ph.D. student in literature, composition, writing, or linguistics, who has been awarded a teaching assistantship, to teach one section of freshman (or first-year) composition, English 401, each semester. Full-time instructors, tenure-track faculty, and adjuncts make up the remainder of the 401 staff. TAs are required to take English 910: Practicum in Teaching College Composition their first semester at UNH. The entire staff attends mandatory, biweekly staff meetings conducted by the head of the department. Numerous contributors reference English 401, the practicum course, and staff meetings.

English 401 classes have a cap of twenty-four students, making it usually the smallest class a student will take his or her freshman year. Although the classes are made up of mostly freshmen, sophomores, nontraditional students in the Division of Continuing Education Program, and nondegree students share space in the roster as well. English 401 is the only course students are required to take by the university. There are approximately seventy sections of the course offered every year.

The students and the university provide the most interesting backdrop by which to contextualize this reader. Established in 1866, UNH is forging its identity as a respected land, sea, and space-grant public research institution. Within its seven schools, there are more than one hundred majors from which undergraduates can choose. The enrollment of undergraduates hovers around 10,500, graduates around 2,000. Sixty percent of the students come from New Hampshire, while another large percentage hail from other New England states. Undeclared Liberal Arts and Business Administration are by far the most highly enrolled programs, and the university boasts an 85 percent first-year retention rate. With an average first year age of 18.4, a 60/40 female to male ratio, a minority distribution of only 3.6 percent and under one hundred undergraduate international students, UNH is an incredibly homogenous university.

Omissions

While we started with a large list of issues that we had wanted to include in this collection, there are, for us, some glaring omissions. Of these, the absence of a deliberate discussion of the presence of race that naturally inhabits our classrooms strikes us as the *most* glaring. We must address the fact that race is indeed present in every encounter with students and in every class that we teach. However, perhaps because of the unique demographics of our university, or an inability to discuss, or anxiety about discussion of it, race as an issue was avoided by all our current contributors. Instead of hounding others to write on race, we hoped that it would find inclusion, as in many of our courses, as an underlying part of the conversation. By doing so, we hope to acknowledge that race is always present in the classroom, regardless of demographics.

Introduction

Silences in Our Teaching Stories: What Do We Leave Out and Why?

Thomas Newkirk

I speak on the phone with my parents, who are both in their late seventies. They tell me about the weather, the flowers, my dad's bird project, the Cleveland Browns—but almost never about a topic I most want to know about, their health.

"How are you feeling, Mom?"

"Fine, fine. I feel all right."

My dad gets angry if I even ask about his health, but, fortunately, each loves to talk about the health of the other. Mom will go on about Dad's bronchitis. My father will describe Mom's knee problem. So the trick is to catch one of them alone in the house. It's a quirk in the Newkirk house, one of many. Do not admit to illness. A silence in the narrative.

I'm interested in the silences in our narratives as teachers, the things we are reluctant to discuss. All groups, it seems to me, construct their own conventions for telling stories, just as my family has done. These conventions define what is said and what is unsaid. They determine the appropriate kinds of responses to certain situations—and they indicate reactions or feelings that are inappropriate. They define the "normal."

Problems occur, though, when we don't feel these "normal feelings," particularly when what we feel is less than noble—anger, envy, frustration, inadequacy, disappointment, or lack of affection. Often in cases like these we remain silent and conclude that there is something wrong with us. To admit these feelings, to tell a different narrative, is to risk being thought weird, perverted, not a good teacher, not a good parent, not a good person.

While I plan to focus on the stories we tell about reading and writing classrooms, I want to begin with a story of motherhood that demonstrates the way we are silenced by conventional cultural myths. The story is called "Myth America" and was written by Karen Weinhold, a participant in the New Hampshire Writing Program.

> For days after the birth of my first child I silently believed that I was an emotional cripple. I felt awe for this new life, tinged with resentment for the intrusion she was making on what little exhausted privacy I had left. But I didn't love her.   .
>
>   When feeding times rolled around I momentarily welcomed the relief from the tedium of the hospital day. Within 10 or 15 minutes I prayed for the nurse to return and take the baby away—I had had enough.

Once at home, I was burdened with the overwhelming responsibility of caring for this squalling bit of humanity. A whole new environment filled with baths, bottles, formulas, diapers, and cradle cap and navel infections insulated me.

Nagging constantly subsurface was my lack of emotional attachment to this child, and I began to seriously consider that I was emotionally unbalanced. Of course, I did not share these feelings with anyone; that would have been totally un-American!

I believed in TV commercials that depicted mother and child rocking in worlds of billowing sheer curtains, sun streaming through quiet dawnings, confidently using the Baby X nurser to achieve this serenity. However, the reality I was living was a grotesque parody of this tranquil scene. The baby woke in the pitch black of night and my body resisted waking, sagging and devoid of maternal joy.

The situation was made worse by unsolicited advice of older women telling Karen that the time of caring for an infant was the best time of a woman's life. For almost three months, Karen carried on this subterfuge, pretending to feel delight.

Then one day, when she was 11 weeks old, it happened. Quite suddenly, out of nowhere, while I sat on the living room floor watching her in her infant's seat, a smile spread her lips as we made eye contact, and my heart vaulted. It was that simple. There it was . . . what I had been searching for since her birth jumped out and grabbed me. . . . I was amazed.

I spent several days puzzling over this phenomena until the truth hit me over the head. It was not possible for me to love or hate something until I knew it. Even predisposition couldn't create these feelings. Until I had tended to her needs, watching her responses increasing daily under my care, and until I had slowly recognized the emerging personality, detachment prevailed. . . .

I wanted to sing and dance and shout the news to the world. I was not emotionally deranged, merely a late bloomer. The myth of instantaneous maternal love, perpetuated by the media, had been dispelled.

In fact, Karen did not immediately shout her discovery to the world. It was years after the birth of the child that she managed to tell outsiders about the experience. Her story was difficult to tell because it was not the conventional mother-love story.

This is just one of many possible examples of the ways women, historically, are asked to emulate perfection: moral perfection—the perfect nurturer willing to expend any amount of energy for friends and family; physical perfection—matching the images of women in the media, always thin, young, and on the edge of sexual adventure; or, more recently, the image of superwoman—seamlessly combining the roles of household manager, caring mother, loving and passionate wife, and dedicated professional.

These ideals, to the extent that they are unrealistic, inflict psychological damage; they induce guilt, envy, and a sense of inadequacy. A friend of mine compared the situation to Margaret Atwood's book, *The Handmaid's Tale,* where there are two classes of women and it was not always clear who belonged to which class. When my friend sees a woman who seems to be managing career and family, she looks for what she calls a "crack," some kind of lapse. Twinkies *and* Doritos in the packed lunch. A rainy Sunday with the kids fighting when the woman screams she can't take it any more, or breaking a glass in the sink in anger. Once this crack appears, my friend knows they can be friends.

As I read the literature on whole language/writing process classrooms, I wonder if we are not creating the role of "super teacher," one more ideal, without cracks, that creates a sense of inadequacy in all of us. Are there silences in the narratives we tell of our whole language/writing process classrooms? Are we telling everything? Do these consistently upbeat success stories capture the emotional underlife of teaching? I think not.

I confess that I have become increasingly estranged from much of what I now read. There is an emotional turbulence and a frequency of failure in my own teaching that I do not see reflected in many accounts, including ones I have written or edited myself. In the classes I read about, everything seems to work; student writing is impressive, often deeply moving; the teacher seems to have achieved full participation of all members of the class. And, what I find most difficult to believe, the teacher never shows signs of despondency, frustration, anger, impatience, or disappointment. If there is anger or frustration, it is directed at external forces—administrators, testing services, the government (the designated "bad guys")—but never at themselves or their students. The teachers I read about don't doubt their competence, or at least they don't admit to their doubts.

I have all these feelings—mixed with exaltation, pride, affection, and admiration, to be sure. But the dark side is there. There are days when I feel the energy sucked out of me, days in late November when I'm teaching a 4:00 freshman English class. It's that time the Scots call the "gloaming," no longer daylight, but not yet night. Still too early to light a fire. Usually a student turns on the lights, but on some days, the first six or seven students just come in and sit in the growing darkness, exhausted; they don't talk. I come into the room and feel as if there is a great weight I must move, and I'm not always sure I can do it. Sometimes I can't. I think of optimistic claims that all students want to write, need to write—and I think, maybe, but not today.

These days of gloaming are hard enough to deal with, but they are much harder if I feel that no one else experiences what I experience, if I imagine their classes getting off to a sparkling beginning, or if I imagine that they never have the sinking feeling that I am experiencing. If I must imagine myself alone with this problem, my very competence as a teacher is called into doubt.

By now you may sense my own paranoia and insecurity—which is fine. As a non-Catholic I have always been fascinated by the act of confession. As a Presbyterian, I was told to do my talking directly to God, but the distance seemed too great. The closest thing I experience to confession, now, is my semiannual trip to the dentist where I'm asked if I floss regularly and I must admit, eyes averted, that I don't. I plan to continue here in this confessional vein, hopeful that there will be some glimmers of recognition in what I say, but recognizing that by the end you may find me a true neurotic.

I'd like to tell a failure story. It is a story about a student that I will call Lisa who took my freshman English class. A goalie on the women's hockey team, and outspoken and responsive in class, Lisa demonstrated real skill in her early assignments in the class—even though she hadn't had much success in high school as a writer.

For one of the early in-class writings, I read a passage from Russell Baker's autobiography, *Growing Up,* describing a teacher, Mr. Fleagle, who generally failed to hold the classes' attention, but who helped Baker discover his ability to write essays. I asked Lisa, and others in the class, to think about a teacher who had affected them. Lisa picked an English teacher, Mrs. Jill Howard, who had earned the nickname "Jill-basa" at a pep rally. Here is how Lisa described it:

Before the time I did at Conant Regional High School, cheerleaders hesitated to set foot inside our gym. Having no cheerleaders of our own, the occupants of our high school took great delight in making basketball games a living hell for any daring squad accompanying an opposing team. Despite the fact that we didn't have any cheerleaders, our principal insisted that pep rallies were a necessity to inspire a basketball team to the coveted title of state champions.

During one of these infamous pep rallies, some of the men in the teaching staff thought it would be funny, if not inspiring, to dress as cheerleaders and cheer for the team. Mrs. Howard would probably have handled the idea of three grown men parading in front of a huge mob of screaming kids, wearing mini-skirts and wigs. But when these men blew up balloons and stuck them up their already tight sweaters, Mrs. Howard was driven into another one of her women's rights campaigns. She was outraged. The straw that broke the camel's back was when one of the teachers, in an attempt to be cute, turned the balloons so that the stems pointed out, achieving the "bra-less" look.

She flew out of the bleachers and pointed out to the superintendent how immature and disrespectful her male cohorts were being. The superintendent tried to accuse her of taking things too personally and told her she should loosen up a little. Then she began yelling, "If you think a woman's mammary glands are so funny, would you be amused if I paraded in front of the student body with a Kielbasa down my pants?"

In her fury Mrs. Howard failed to notice that she was screaming in the direction of the microphone. The entire gym was silent as Mrs. Howard made her point. The men in the cheerleader outfits were not willing to be humiliated that easily, thus Jill Howard was dubbed "Jill-basa."

... I had great admiration for the way she stood up against the entire school. When I hear her good-naturedly being called "Jill-basa" by a fellow staff member, or behind her back by some wise ass student, I have nothing but respect for her.

I admired the same thing in Lisa's writing that she admired in Mrs. Howard. I liked her boldness, her clear feminist point of view (not common among New Hampshire eighteen-year-olds). I liked the way she could snap off this anecdote. Based on this paper, and her next one on what it was like to play goalie for the *boys'* hockey team at her high school, I sensed (and I think she sensed) her skill as a writer. It seemed like it might be one of those rare times when a student finds a major, even a vocation.

But things fell apart. In the last part of the course, students were to write one paper involving research and another responding to a novel. Lisa, as I recall, set out to write a fictional account in which she worked in information about steroid use at the University of New Hampshire. I remember my sinking feelings as I read her first draft. The incidents seemed contrived, uninteresting, and she seemed to be presenting no information. I remember suggesting that she interview some of the athletes on the university's sports teams and that she consider not using this fictional approach—because it didn't seem to be working for her. In my enthusiasm, I'm sure my suggestion sounded like direction. My nudge was more of a shove.

The paper never developed; a few bits of information were inserted into her account. And I could feel that the collaborative spirit of our conferences on the early papers was gone. Her work on the last paper was perfunctory. On her evaluation for the course, she complained about me telling her how her papers should be written, rather than allowing her to write the paper she wished to write. It was painful to read at the time, painful to recount now.

As I thought of my work with Lisa, I realized, now four years later, that I had missed an important clue to working with her. In her paper on becoming a goalie on the male team, she talked about the men—and father and the principal—who had discouraged her from trying to make the team. She wrote about how she had had to ignore their advice, and how she had proved she could handle the job. It is now clear that she saw me as one more man who was trying to divert her from what she wanted to do. She had told me that the great lesson of her life was not to be diverted, and I had missed the warning.

A quick, and I believe faulty, lesson to derive from this failure story is the need to grant the student "ownership," a term that belies the complex relationships we have with students. According to the ownership interpretation, I took over the paper, and the student became alienated from her own writing. In other words, I had neglected one of the basic tenets of the writing process movement. But, in practice, working with students is never so simple as applying basic rules. There are times when I have had to be directive in exactly the same way I was with Lisa. I recall a student who had decided to write a research paper on "Russia" but came back because the library didn't have anything on his topic. That student didn't need me to hang back; he needed some fairly explicit guidance.

In Lisa's case, the issue was much more complex than applying the rule "give students ownership." I had to balance objectives that conflicted in some way. On one hand I wanted her to make choices in her writing and to feel the sense of control that comes with making choices. *I also wanted her to succeed.* The situation became difficult when her choices seemed to be taking her in a direction that, at least to me, would not result in a satisfactory paper. It was a close call—and I blew it.

It was a close call in the way that many of our tough decisions are close calls. Our thirteen-year-old daughter wants to take the bus to an evening movie at the mall. How do we as parents balance our (and her) desire for her to be independent with a concern for her safety? We say no. But it was close. If many of our decisions as teachers are close calls, it is inevitable that we will often make the wrong choice. But who writes about these close calls, these decisions we would like to have back? If all I hear is complacent silence, do I conclude I am the only one with regrets?

I'd like to suggest some ways we can tell new stories that explore the issues the success stories leave out.

1. Create forums for telling failure stories. We all have them. Let's talk about them. At the staff meetings at the University of New Hampshire we found that we were trapped in success stories—everything worked. So one day we scheduled a meeting we entitled "Bombs." Everybody had to come with a failure story, and we began with the most experienced staff, including the director.

2. There is another kind of story, related to the failure story, that may be even more important for our psychic balance—the story we tell to celebrate absurdity. These stories are not necessarily about failure, but about the ways in which our teaching doesn't always work out the way we planned. Here's one from the early writing process research that Don Graves conducted.

A first grader, I'll call her Emily, had just finished her story on her birthday party. It went something like this: "I had a party. It was fun. We did lots of things." The teacher, schooled in appropriate response, said, "It sounds like your party was fun"—and then began to probe. What kinds of things did you do? Did you have a cake? What kind? What was your favorite present? After Emily supplied a few answers, the teacher said, "Don't you think a reader would want to know these things?"

Emily replied, "I've got an idea. If some people in the class want to know more about my parties, I'll invite them to the next one." She closed her book and didn't add a word.

Stories like these keep us sane and humble. We laugh—but at the same time are reminded that things don't always work as we planned. They celebrate the unpredictability of teaching. For me, they are that "crack" I spoke of earlier, the opening that allows for companionship.

3. Teachers should regularly visit the classes of other teachers. When I was teaching high school I was appalled at how little cross-classroom visiting went on. I imagined that elementary schools, because they were smaller, did a better job at this. I'm now convinced I was wrong. In most schools there seems to be almost no visiting. Districts seem far more willing to let teachers come to conventions where we can talk in airless rooms at some remove about teaching.

   Visiting helps us all learn new ways of teaching, and, I feel, it also can give us more realistic models of success than we get from the success stories that we read. I remember when the first work on the writing process was coming out, with all the kids loving to write all the time. I had trouble picturing the classroom. It didn't sound like any classrooms I'd been in. When I visited one of the project classrooms, there were a couple of boys playing in the sandbox during writing time. I'm not suggesting it wasn't a fine and innovative class. It was. But I was so grateful, so relieved to see those boys—who could care less about writing—in the sandbox.

4. Finally, those of us who write and make presentations about writing can try to be more balanced in the examples of student work we present. I know from experience that the temptation to highlight extraordinary work is almost irresistible, particularly if we are trying to convince people that our approach works. But I feel we can do a better job by showing some less than exemplary examples, too.

I would like to mention one book that has told these new stories better than any other book I know—Sondra Perl and Nancy Wilson's *Through Teachers' Eyes*. The book is a collection of portraits of teachers who had worked in a writing project. The authors made the bold move of describing a successful teacher, Ross Burkhardt, who had a bad year. He never established a good working relationship with the students. The more things did not seem to work the more he pressed; the more he pressed the worse the relationship became. At the end of the year a student wrote, "I think you shouldn't get as close [to the class] as you were this year because in every class you have there is always someone trying to give you hell." Sondra Perl wrote:

Giving Ross hell. The words stuck...The students had given him a year of hell. They tried his patience, exhausted his will, defeated his spirit. And by the end of the year they had won. On the last day of school, unlike so many years past, Ross organized no final culminating class, wrote no poem to commemorate the occasion, staged no play to perform in—perhaps the most telling sign of defeat. (1986, 144)

In writing Ross's portrait, Perl was faced with a dilemma. Ross learned from his bad year, his style of leadership changed, and he regained the commitment of his students. But Perl had this data from his bad year. She wrote about her problem:

> Yet in those years, as Ross regained his footing, I continued to write about the year he lost it. Occasionally, when I showed him the drafts, I wondered whether he wouldn't have wished that I rewrite history, soften a description, rework a particular incident. Yet throughout all our meetings, Ross was remarkably consistent, saying—and meaning—that if there were something in his struggle that might be of value to other teachers, then I should tell his story as I was doing, no holds barred. Several years later, I am still struck by his willingness to allow me to use his story to serve others. (148)

If we are looking for heroes, I nominate Ross Burkhardt. And I hope that he will be remembered not as the teacher who suffered through a bad year, but as the teacher who wanted the story of that year told—"no holds barred." May we all be as honest in telling the stories of our teaching.

As I was preparing this essay I showed a draft of it to Karen Weinhold, the author of the piece on mother love that I quoted earlier. A couple of weeks later she sent me a draft of an essay about her teaching of writing. Karen had become a major innovator in her district, but the piece focused on peer response groups—they'd never worked well for her. What struck me was the confessional tone of the piece. It was as if she was admitting a sin that she'd kept hidden for years. Groups had never worked well for her. Conferences, yes. But not groups. She'd shared her secret with some of her colleagues, and each of them had a secret, too. One was uncomfortable with teaching absolutely no grammar. Another found her record-keeping system took so much time that she never read on her own. Silences. Secrets.

It's time they stopped being secrets. It's time we tell the whole story of our teaching. No holds barred.

1

"This Is Duct Tape"

Holding It Together During
Your First Semester

If there is a common thread throughout discussions between soon-to-be first-time teachers it is this: uncertainty. Whether it be your first time standing in front of a classroom of students, the first time in a new department, or the first time teaching college-age students, you don't know what to expect, and that can be terrifying.

So we try to start with what we know: ourselves. The days, weeks, months before we step into the classroom for the first time are selfish. We're self-obsessed, self-contained, wondering what the students' first impressions of *us* will be, if *we* will trip, if they will laugh at *us*. What will we wear? What will we say? Will they see that we're just posing as writing teachers? We wonder if we should crack jokes or put on our best librarian suits and strike an authoritative pose. We obsess over the number of times we say "um," the too-fast speech, the grand pauses. And all of this is done only for our own panicked reflections in the mirror. What bag should we carry? What readings are *we* comfortable teaching? What in the world were we *thinking*? Our uncertainty. We're a selfish lot.

We write and rewrite lesson plans, striving for perfection. We plan and replan assignments; we even reinvent our personas in an attempt to be prepared for that first day, that first week, that first month of standing in front of a classroom. But it's difficult to envision the semester as a whole, as a series of learning moments that build upon one another in a writing classroom, when the whole time we're anxious about our authority, about the silences in the classroom, about student behavior, student writing, about where to put your other hand when you write on the board. It's difficult to envision the intricate layers of teaching, when we simply don't know what to expect. We have spent countless years in classrooms, we think, the role of the teacher should seem easy. We have a nagging feeling, though, that the other side of the desk will be much different. In the pages that follow we attempt to provide you with a glimpse behind the big desk. In reading these essays we hope that your upcoming semester becomes a little more clear, and that you are better able to envision yourself standing in front of that classroom, taking it moment by moment, picking yourself up when you fail, and celebrating the moments when you succeed. We know that this isn't a solution to anxiety; think of it (as Carrie Heimer does) as duct tape—something to help hold it all together.

1

Forty-Eight Eyeballs

Carrie Heimer

Forty-eight eyeballs. I know they must be drying out by now. This is just like the staring contests with my past goldfish. I never win. How can they go so long without blinking? It's an optician's dream and my nightmare: the wide-eyed, ceaseless gaze of twenty-four bodies. I feel like one big headlight in a herd of deer. Or maybe it's one small deer in a headlight factory. Either way I'm outnumbered. I should have been a computer scientist.

> Expect to stammer. Expect to stutter. Expect to develop every speech impediment known to humankind overnight.
>
> Expect to mix up their names. Expect to forget their names. Expect to forget your name.
>
> Expect to hide in the bathroom for the seven minutes and sixteen seconds before class. Expect to drop your pen. Repeatedly. Expect to forget your shoes.

The first class session of freshman composition. We read Hughes' "Theme for English B" thoroughly and model it in a freewrite. The fifth student to share his freewrite unleashed a diatribe against poetry, modeling after other writers, reading his work aloud, and listening to others' freewrites. It goes on. He's written for fifteen minutes, lambasting every possible element of the class with the exclusion of my clothing and the room number. I have to say something. He sits with smug satisfaction plastered all over his face. (I want to write "acne-ridden face," but that would be shameless retribution, and what's worse, it's not even accurate.) The ball is in my court. I've never taught this class before. I haven't had much opportunity to brainstorm with other instructors about it because everyone else is just as busy as I am, and they seem busier. I don't want to ask how to teach the class I self-assuredly said I would teach, and I don't want to be standing here while my new students all sense a Springer moment brewing. Some look embarrassed and apologetic for this vitriolic outburst from their ranks. Some look delighted at the brave soul bucking the system, giving it to whatever they perceive "the man" or "the system" to be. I even suspect that some of them believe I represent this system, that I am somehow identified with the woman that gave them a hard time in financial aid, or the man that ticketed their cars this morning for forgetting to feed the meters. Only one or two compassionate faces seem to understand that I have stood in the same lines they have, and that I know how outrageous the notebook prices are in the bookstore. I'm the same as they are, and all I want to do is steal into my seat and wait for the real professor to breeze in drenched in confidence and take this uncomfortable situation in hand. Because I can't think of anything else to do, I applaud.

I've been telling a friend for months that I'm going to learn a quick soft-shoe routine to break out when I can't get "off" any other way. Teaching is the only production that doesn't give you a clean exit, an inviting offstage darkness, an immediate and well-timed invisibility. Dozens of times, I've longed to leave the classroom after a good laugh or zinger that garnered ooohs and aaahs even from the stoic students. Unfortunately, there's no alternative but to keep standing there, keep pacing that eight-foot space in front of the desk you might sit at or sit on, wondering each time you do whether you're earning "hip" points or just showing off your slip or the mismatched socks you figured would stay hidden under the respectable trousers. A quiet sigh is my private lament for the perfect out that passes me by too early in the class to let them go.

My office is small and slants drastically into a low corner. It feels like a burrow, and that isn't an inappropriate image for the five minutes left before every class. The five minutes when I could go in early and make strained small talk with the uncomfortable and rare early students. The five minutes when I could try to sketch out whatever notes we'll need on the chalkboard and transparently overlook the students already waiting. The five minutes when I could more simply hole up in my office watching seconds dwindle off of my watch. What is my model for what I "should" do as a "good" teacher? Rumor and legend. Maybe I ought to sit in other classrooms for those five minutes and then leave when it's time for my own to begin. Then I could witness first-hand the choices of the more experienced. But all I get is fantastic, inspiring, utterly intimidating rumor of the easy banter so and so has with her class, or the legend of the way the most dynamic professor opened his class sessions. Where do I find my norms for this experience and how carefully do I interrogate them before I accept them? What do I really believe about what it is I'm supposed to be doing?

The first staff meeting as a graduate student: I recognize one or two other graduate students, either seasoned veterans with an entire semester under their belts, or others who feel like they, too, have suddenly infiltrated the faculty lounge and are soon to be discovered as frauds. I've already picked up my mail in the department cubby that clearly reads "No Students Allowed" and feel sort of deviant and guilty over the breach. The discussion is on first class sessions or writing a syllabus or a first assignment, which is ideal, except that I've already distributed mine or given the assignment or blown the first impression as approachable yet knowledgeable, sensitive yet rigorous, entertaining yet no-nonsense, and most of all commanding, firm, and fueled with a passion for all things written, all beauty, all truth. The perfect presidential candidate. Instead, I turned sixty-eight shades of red and tripped over an extension cord. Now I'm here to listen to accomplished, published, tenured professors and instructors give off-the-cuff pointers and laugh over those days long past when they were awkward or bumbling. What was fifteen years ago for them was two days ago for me. I feel incapable, inadequate, and shy, and my slanting burrow looks pretty good right now. Welcome to your normative community.

On top of the unrealistic expectations I construct for myself by listening only to the stellar skills of others, pile the slew of movies my students and I have all seen and added to our storehouse of impressions about what should happen in the classroom. I've failed repeatedly to be Robin Williams in *Dead Poet's Society* and my students know it. Neither am I the imposing paternal figure in an inner city in *Lean On Me*. I don't carry a baseball bat and I can't quote as much Whitman as I might like or impersonate John Wayne. Frankly, I'm in a position of authority rather suddenly, though perhaps I've never identified myself as the teaching "type," and I waver between the smugness of mastery in my subject, and the ego-crushing blow of a flip student asking without thinking, "How old *are* you? Have you done this before?"

There are devastating moments when I realize that crashing, burning failure of my perceived goals in my first semester. After absorbing the mythologies of the creative and unruffled, I have set goals such as: inspire in each student a new passion for interpreting meaning and crafting language; connect in a profound and personal but professional way with each student; lead each student to the completion of a stunning essay dealing with significant personal material, potentially things they haven't been able to work out yet in years of counseling; open the door to the rest of their writing lives in such a way that they see it and appreciate it; value each student equally and objectively as a writer and thinker. Set against those goals is the day I realize, to my mortification, that I dislike one of my students intensely. Horror! Or the day I recognize in myself the acute desire to be in bed watching *Casino* instead of standing in front of my class in ten minutes. Abomination! Or the day I sit face to face with a student in conference and blank out entirely, dredging and digging, but finding nothing whatever to say about the essay before us, constructive or otherwise. What's worse, I'm actually distracted enough to notice that the student is wearing an excess of cologne. Outrage! These dreadful epiphanies peel away layer after layer of ill-fitted motivation until I find myself staring in the mirror wondering if I could write down three good reasons I'm teaching or three things I believe about what I really want to do over a semester.

Here is what I believe about the Super-Instructors in every composition program: they can give you three reasons why they teach. It doesn't need to be more than three. Sometimes it doesn't even need to be as many as three. But they can give you those reasons. Their reasons. I wish I could say I've asked more people about their reasons. Maybe writing it down will remind me to do so. But the reason I'll ask will be to hear insights, no norms. No one else stands in my classroom. Rarely, if ever, does anyone even visit. So why should their reasons be on my syllabus, or hanging in my office? My honest goals and motivations are more valuable than a thousand perfect exercises because they fit. On the flip side, another truth about Super-Instructors: they learn to have simple conversations with their peers about what works. More often than not, that isn't a fully premeditated and flawlessly executed foundation and joinery; that's duct tape. There needn't be less integrity to a good quick fix. Super-Instructors seem to love identifying with fellow educators, and they also seem to get tired. Super-Instructors rest and rely, rejuvenate and regroup. In short, no Super-Instructor really believes she's a Super-Instructor. But she knows, in those five minutes before class, that she is doing no worse than anyone else.

It's stand-up comedy meets gladiator sports. My students, in the middle of a four-year mood swing and desperate search for norms that I understand all too well, are mercurial enough to go from a crowd of bloodthirsty Romans to an appreciative, even fawning audience in the space of a week. And what do I want in the middle of all this? In the midst of essays on binge drinking, dying grandparents, the Apple Harvest festival in Old Town Square, first sex? This crazed spectrum of the innocent and indulgent? I want desperately to conduct a successful workshop. This is where I step back and laugh. Would I really feel fulfilled as a teacher if my students sat in their attentive circle and reported vigorously on the image pattern in an essay on Muhammed Ali or shopping? The rewarding moments are when my students let me discover that they are in the same wrestling ring I am. I get a glimpse of the little man behind the curtain, so to speak, and get to step up and guide others who are in the market for brains, hearts, courage. I can't provide these things. Neither can the study of composition. But I can help package the request.

The last session of freshman composition. A student approaches me tentatively with her final piece, a personal essay written in flashbacks and vignettes. She hesitates about turning it in because she's never written in this style before. She hesitates about turning it in because it's the first time she's written about a controlling father.

> Expect to tap dance for an audience of one. Expect to be more graceful than you thought. Expect to hear clapping from people you didn't think were watching.
>
> Expect to laugh. Expect to grimace. Expect to be known.
>
> Expect to be an inexperienced teacher. Expect to be a self-conscious teacher. Expect to be an effective teacher.

2

My Imagined Community

Anne Bramblett

I shove my feet into my worn shoes wondering how the humidity in New Hampshire could be as oppressive as it is in Virginia. Bad winters, bad summers, I grumble as I head for the indoor gym. My feet hit the whirling tread, Bruce Springsteen's raspy voice sings of escape and broken dreams through my earphones. Soon the monotonous repetition of movement and the humming of the tread beneath my feet put me in a trance. I begin to focus on teaching. I am twenty-two, recently accepted as a graduate student in English literature at the University of New Hampshire. My thoughts turn to the first day as a writing instructor. I look at my reflection in the windowpane; my eyes focus further. I begin to rehearse, the trees my first audience. I draw a short breath as I realize that in less than a month the assembly of trees will be replaced by twenty-four composition students.

Today I try a new role. I am the fun young teaching assistant. We critique Britney Spears' new music video; we swap predictions of *Felicity*'s season premiere. I am their peer and potentially their friend and confidante. I promise the class discussions will be outrageous, the writing in the course passionate and profound. I know tomorrow my part will be much different. I will become the green scholar, my rank in the university elusive. I will be studious: I don my glasses, my hair is upswept. I promise that we will work hard; the writing will be intensive and highly rewarding.

Effortlessly, I can see the common thread of my treadmill ruminations: my first day is always a success, no matter whom I decide to be. My students are amiable, eager to get to know each other and me. They are gregarious and committed to being part of a community of learners. I project my ideal students into my ideal classroom setting. I am, of course, the ideal teacher.

My idealism is reflected in the course objectives I outline in my syllabus: "Throughout the semester," I begin confidently, we will approach writing, reading and researching as a means to analyze our own histories and realities, critique our culture, and, most importantly, to place ourselves in a broader cultural context. I hope that you use the relatively safe environment of the freshman writing course to take risks in both your thinking and your writing. We will be asking many difficult questions, many of which you will explore in your papers, and it is my hope that you will leave with many more.

I want my classroom to focus on relevant cultural topics such as gender identity, consumerism, images and representations of America, and the role of education in their lives. I am eager to be a part of, and witness to a coming to voice, personal growth, and a questioning of previously held ideology. I realize, however, that to aid my students in their critical reading, writing, and thinking, I have to rely on their verbal involvement in class. I outline my participation expectations in my syllabus:

> As much as this is a writing intensive course, it is also *discussion-heavy.* The success of this class is directly related to your involvement: you will be expected to render public your thoughts, ideas, opinions, and interests. I will take on the responsibility of launching discussions and planning class activities (though, theoretically, by the end of the semester the class will be responsible for aiding in the class's development). You are here to develop a voice through writing, participation in class discussions, and the oral sharing of your work. I will expect that you come to class engaged in the assigned reading and committed to the quality of the course by participating.

My expectations are high, but I don't think unreasonable. I recall my own freshman year of college—the large lecture halls, the stoic, intimidating professors. My course is designed as a refuge from their other classes—it is centered on workshopping, not lecturing. I want to give my students an opportunity to develop relationships with their classmates as well as with me; I will facilitate peer workshop groups, assemble both small and full-class discussion groups, meet with my students in biweekly conferences. My goal is to encourage and foster a community of writers, thinkers, researchers, and readers.

The boundaries of my imagined community began to take form the previous December as I wrote my University of New Hampshire Teaching Assistant application:

> In classes where everyone sits in a circle, fostering a community atmosphere, students have more of a responsibility to talk, to react, and to find their voice. There is no better place for dialogue than in a writing classroom. It is in the democratic classroom that effective writing skills are learned; the realization that voice in class can be transformed into a voice on paper is empowering for students discovering the potential of language.

I believe I can model my pedagogy by assigning a personal essay early in the semester. My imagined community becomes steeped in the feminist mantra:

the personal is the political. I can model through the personal essay the essential ingredients of critical thinking: examination and analysis. In order for my students to leave the class questioning the institutions that entrench them, they must first come to voice through expressing, examining, questioning, and analyzing their own experiences. "When developing a community of writers," I continued in my application:

> I will want to ensure an environment that will foster a voice both in class and on paper. If students feel comfortable and appreciated, as when one honestly listens to their ideas in class, they will find their voices and shape them in their papers. "Coming to voice," bell hooks states in *Teaching to Transgress: Education as the Practice of Freedom*, "is not just the act of telling one's experiences. It is using that telling strategically—to come to voice so that you can also speak freely about other subjects" (1994, 148). The confidence acquired through a community environment leads students to self- and cultural examination, modeling critical thinking techniques.

I quickly snap out of my thoughts, my endless what-ifs, my infinite roles, when I walk into my classroom the first day realizing my only shield against the moving mass of unknown bodies is my assurance that after fifteen weeks they will "come to voice." They will be astonished as I, layer by layer, unveil their ideology. They will gawk when I expose the simulacra. They will not be able to stop their pens when questioning their role in the university, the cultural formation of gender roles and expectations, racial stereotypes, and the ethical practices of the titans of industry. What they *did* do, however, was sit and stare—their mouths sewn shut—unable to communicate with me or with each other. My confidence as well as the foundation of my imagined community crumbled with the weight of the silence of my classroom.

Certainly, I wasn't alone in my idealism. My colleagues, as well as sharing my anxiety, were also highly idealistic about the success of their classes. Everyone seemed confident during our TA orientation, appearing relaxed while we bonded over pizza. I was reluctant to talk about my anxiety in the face of such a calm group. I found in my practicum course I was hesitant to discuss my failure in the classroom. Colleagues swapped stories of success: the suave, off-the-cuff remarks that reformed resistant students, the fearlessness and expertise in administering poor grades, the hilarious remarks of loquacious students.

I always harbored a curious pity for and awe of Charlie Brown. The swinging of the leg against the air, the thump of a round body landing on its back, Lucy's mirth when Charlie looked up to see the football pressed hard against her chest. I felt just like Charlie Brown every time I walked into the classroom, took a quick swing at a class discussion, only to fall flat on my back. Yet every day, I would straighten my clothes, brush off the dirt and try again. Fail again—with the hope that *this time* I would succeed. When I thought I couldn't bear the silence and failure one more day, I decided that I would enlist the help of my practicum course classmates.

I've been struggling, I confessed to my fellow TAs, since the first day of class to get my students to participate in small and full-class discussions. I thought I had found the panacea—we would watch an episode of *The Simpsons* that tied into the personal essays they were reading as well as writing. Their assignment was to write about their identities—an experience or expertise that defined them. It was as if the episode had been written with me and my class in mind: Lisa Simpson's identity of the smart, talented girl of Springfield Elementary is jeopardized by the arrival of an equally intelligent and talented girl. I was excited; I was confident that this exercise would do the trick—my class would laugh together, would want to talk about *The Simpsons,* to make connections between their writing on identity and the episode's identity theme. I launched into my first question—"so what did y'all think?"—only to realize in horror that my plan had failed: their eyes were averted, their bodies slouched deep into their chairs, a pen rolled slowly behind one finger, over the next, repeatedly.

Suddenly my classroom community became a hackneyed scene from a Sunday Western. It was me against them, staring as we fingered our guns. Who would the silence break first? I began to rock in my chair; the incessant squeak, I believed, would drive anyone crazy enough to talk. Silence. Teacher time is unique—a fifty-minute class can seem only fifteen minutes when the momentum is strong. But when you're faced with silence, you can either "Bueller" your way out of it and move on, or you can wait it out. The wait seems endless. They had won—I told them they could leave.

What do I do with a class that is reluctant to talk to each other and thereby fails to fulfill my expectations of a community of scholars interested in questioning their assumptions? My colleagues eagerly offered brilliant suggestions: get them into small groups more often, give them the chance to bond, wait out the silence longer, talk to the students individually about their lack of participation, increase participation points in the final grade.

Using their advice, I began to take a more active role in constructing a classroom discussion. I no longer thought I could depend on opening the floor to discussion (with a pathetic "what did y'all think?") and expect the class to explode with ideas, interpretations, and opinions. I needed a backup plan, and I came to class prepared with a list of questions about the readings but was always willing to abandon any predetermined path of conversation if the class decided to set its own course. I asked them to write a one-page reading response every day they had a reading assignment due, allowing them to use their own writing as a discussion cue. I would incorporate into the discussion the five required questions about the piece that they turned in at the beginning of class.

As the semester progressed, and I began to know my students on a more personal level (conferences became as much getting to know my students personally as they were a way to talk about writing), I realized that my best "beat-the-silence" weapon was my memory. If a student had written an essay that related to the reading we were discussing, I would ask the student to talk about what she wrote about. The student was immediately validated—I thought her ideas were important enough to share and remember. By simply showing that I was *listening* to their stories and experiences in and out of class as well as reading their essays closely, they were more willing to rip the seams from their mouths and *speak*.

Even now, after completing my Master's degree and receiving a job as an instructor at UNH, I am still unsure of the definition of an "ideal classroom discussion." It seems an elusive abstraction that I strive to meet every day, one that on the treadmill Augusts ago, I would have imagined only my success at meeting, yet now I never allow myself to believe I can truly achieve it. I refuse to relax in the comfort of familiar activities, readings, and writing assignments. In the pursuit of the cure for the silent classroom I have discovered the sublimity of failure and of failure narrowly averted. The terror of silence allows me to take the risks in my teaching that I expect in my students' writing. It is only within the experience of failure, then, that my classroom can move closer to what I envision as a community of writers.

3

Waiting for Surprise

Michael J. Michaud

One of the most frustrating experiences I've had teaching freshman composition is reading essays that can't pass what Donald Murray would call the no-surprise-for-the-writer-no-surprise-for-the-reader test. In these essays, students usually tell the story of a "significant moment" in their life and then attempt to impose some sort of "moral" or "life lesson" upon the story (or sometimes impose none at all). What makes these essays unsatisfying is the fact that, at the moment when the student put pen to paper or finger to keyboard, he or she already knew the outcome of the story and had usually already processed the moral or life lesson, which was gleaned from the significant moment.

When I read such an essay, I can usually tell by the end of the first paragraph where the essay is headed and what the message will be. If I encountered it in a more professional context, meaning if the student's essay appeared in a magazine or journal or newspaper, I would stop reading at the conclusion of the first paragraph, at the point when I realized that nothing new or surprising was going to be unveiled. But since I am their teacher and it is my job to help them become better writers, I must keep reading.

There are many subgenres within the no-surprise-for-the-writer-no-surprise-for-the-reader genre. One subgenre in which I have become especially interested is an essay I've come to call the *sports narrative*. Always written by former athletes and usually written by males (but increasingly popular among female students as well), the sports narrative comes in a variety of shapes and sizes. It concerns itself with some kind of adversity the student conquered on the playing field or arena, usually during high school. Its setting is the BIG season, the BIG game, or the BIG play. Its "moral" or "life lesson" is predictable and ranges from "this experience taught me that no matter the obstacle, you should never stop reaching for your goals" to "from this experience I learned that anything is possible with teamwork." These messages are positive, optimistic, forward-looking, unambiguous themes that we try to teach our children in an effort to unleash their potential. The fact that so many of my students write essays that center around the importance of teamwork and overcoming adversity seems to confirm that Little League and varsity coaches alike are getting their messages across. In fact, if I were a parent, I would be proud to have a son or daughter compose an essay that shows the way he or she learned the value of hard work and team effort.

So why is it, I wonder each time I receive another sports narrative, that I *cannot stand* reading such essays?

All my life I have been an athlete. Growing up in a small, white-bread, Reagan–Republican-loving town in northern California, and then a conservative suburb northwest of Chicago, I learned to love competition. My life was cyclical—divided not by the change of seasons, but rather, by the arena in which I performed when the seasons changed. My identity was inextricably bound to a vision of myself as an athlete, a performer: a runner, thrower, hitter, catcher, kicker, jumper, swinger. In the summer I swam and played tennis. In the fall, I played soccer. In the winter, basketball. And in the spring, I was absorbed by baseball—the intoxicating elixir of cut grass, the warm scent of ballpark hot dogs, and the sweet, sweet smell of sweat and dirt mixed with cotton. With my bat-bag slung over my shoulder and my glove dangling from the handlebars, I pedaled my bike to the field for Little League tryouts in mid-April. The coaches picked the teams and the season was underway. I learned how to run and throw and slide, how to field a ground ball so that I didn't take it on the chin, how to turn a double play and hit the cutoff man from left field when throwing from the fence.

As I worked my way through middle school and then high school, my life was comprised of one contest of physical skill after another. Sure, school was important, but it wasn't the place from whence I drew my sense of self-worth, identity, values. In my world, the measure of a boy was taken among other boys and men, on the field or court, in the pool or at the rink—the performance was public and the nature of the performance was physical. The goal was clear: to work hard, to win.

After high school I went off to college and a turmoil-filled year and a half as a business major. The courses in the business college—calculus, macro- and microeconomics, business statistics—simply didn't excite me and so I finally switched my major to English, knowing full well that it wouldn't guarantee me a job after college, but sure that I couldn't study business any longer. As an English major, I began to learn a new set of values and a different kind of performance. I was no longer the athlete, I was now the bookworm, or more generously, the scholar. The performance upon which I was evaluated was still public, but it was no longer physical and it demanded more of me than simply working hard or winning. In my new performance, I had to present what Thomas Newkirk, in his book, *The Performance of Self in Student Writing,* would call a different "self." According to Newkirk, in order to write a successful personal essay "the writer needs to present a more malleable self, one that can be 'affected' significantly by experience" (1997, 22). The kind of personal essays freshman

English teachers want, Newkirk explains, shows the writer in a "staged process of self-actualization" (1997, 22). As an English major, I learned, and had to demonstrate, that I understood the values of the academy, the writer, the scholar: that I could ask myself questions and not necessarily seek answers, that I could observe myself and the world around me in order to better understand why I'm here, that I could imagine the experiences of people unlike myself and gain the capacity for empathy, and that I could appreciate irony and complexity. In short, I had to learn how to be curious again. In my literature classes, I wrote essays about the ideas I encountered in the strange books I was asked to read, books that no one in my family had ever read and my friends had never heard of. In my writing classes, I wrote short stories and personal essays in which I attempted to make sense of my life and the world around me. I learned a new kind of performance and I performed.

In graduate school I discovered Donald Murray for the first time through his book *Write to Learn.* "I write to discover, to be surprised, to experience, to find out; I write to learn," Murray states (1999, 5), and for the first time I began to understand what it was my professors in college were trying to show me: that writing can be a tool or a vehicle, or a means by which individuals better understands themselves, their worlds, or some given topic (1999, 5). It was a revelation to discover the theory behind what I had been practicing for the past several years as an undergraduate.

It would be hard to pinpoint exactly when I first allowed myself to discover what I had to say through the act of writing. But here's the important thing: I'm pretty sure—actually, almost *positive*—I *didn't* learn how to discover what I had to say in my first writing course, Freshman English 401, at the University of New Hampshire. I'm pretty sure that, like the students I teach today, I wrote sports narratives about my experience playing tennis or basketball or baseball in high school. I also wrote essays about the friends I had left behind and the difficulty of making the transition to college life. I'm almost positive, looking back, that my 401 instructor encouraged me to free-write and to "not plan" my writing, but I'm pretty sure I didn't really grasp the concept.

In high school, I had learned what most students learn about writing: that it is for analyzing books, poems, and stories that you may or may not have read, that it is for telling the teacher the answer so that you might earn a high grade, and that it is for telling stories about your life that reveal that you are a good and moral person. Like so many of my students today, I had learned one single model for conceptualizing the way writing works. I was to know where I was going, know what I was going to say, and say it clearly. It's not surprising, then, that like many of my students, when I got to college and began to write essays (I certainly didn't understand what it meant *to essay*—to attempt or to try—at that point) I failed to make the paradigm shift in thinking about writing that my instructor may have been advocating.

So where does all this leave me, as an instructor, today? At times I've thought about simply banning essays like the sports narrative from my classroom. But the problem isn't really with the sports narrative. The sports narrative is merely an example of the larger difficulty of writing what we, as instructors of English, see as meaningful essays. If I believe a long line of composition theorists, meaningful essays, in their completed form, do two things. One, they say something that I, as the reader, did not expect to read. Two, they say something in a way that, previously, I had never heard. Now, how do I get my eighteen-year-old students who are away from home for the first time, trying to find a way to manage their time so they don't fall behind in their studies, trying to meet new friends while still keeping in contact with the old, trying to figure out what they want to be when they grow up, trying to find the best party on the weekend, and trying to find someone with whom to establish intimacy, to do those two things and not write essays like the sports narrative, which, in my eyes, are predictable and unsatisfying?

The answer is, I wait. And while I'm waiting, I try to be more patient with those sports narratives. After all, when my students and I gather in workshops to discuss their work, they don't usually find each other's essays predictable, as I do. When one student writes a sports narrative and we discuss it in workshop, the other students often share stories of their own experiences with high school athletics that echo the narrative under examination. They talk about their own BIG season or BIG game or BIG play—the games they too won or failed to win, the team on which they played that finally came together or never did. They are surprised by their shared experience and, in their eyes, their peers' essays often *do* say something they did not expect to read, in a way they did not expect to read it.

Even with a renewed sense of patience, I don't expect that my frustration over receiving sports narratives, or similar essays, in my first-year writing courses is going to dissipate any time soon. But I have learned this: that to expect my students will learn how to "surprise" themselves in writing—how to make discoveries *through* the act of writing—in one semester, when it took me several years to learn is simply unrealistic. Like my students, I, too, will have to wait for the surprise to come, and while I won't give up on the importance of discovery and surprise in a piece of writing, and I won't give up trying to foster it in my students' work, I won't be so disappointed if, in the span of a single fifteen-week semester, it doesn't come.

4

Minimum Requirements

Alison Knoblauch

Before I got to New Hampshire I hadn't seen the ocean. It's true. I'm from Wisconsin, born and raised (no ocean there), and this fourteen-hundred mile move to graduate school was, well, a bit intimidating. As you can imagine, I was worried about pretty much everything: would I like the apartment? Would I have enough money? Would I do okay in my classes? Would New Hampshire have cheese? Would we get the Packer games? But my most nagging concern, the one that kept me up at night, had to do with teaching.

I was a secondary education major throughout most of my undergraduate career, until I started to spend some time in the middle and high schools. I hated it. I mean really hated it. Why? I guess I've seen *Dead Poet's Society* one too many times. See, I had this idea that I would swagger (yes, swagger) into the classroom and *inspire* my students. Okay, maybe not all my students, but somewhere along the line at least a few of them would realize the joy in literature, the sheer beauty of the written word. They would "ooh ooh ooh" when I asked for volunteers to read the part of Lady Macbeth. I was totally unprepared for the reality of teaching high school. So I switched my major and did what I knew that I really wanted to do: teach college. I would soon find that I was completely unprepared for the reality of teaching at the college level as well.

Here's the thing. If you're in graduate school, and if you're going to be teaching college students, chances are someone believes that you're a good student. Whether you admit it or not, you probably believe that you're a good student too. Yet at the same time, you don't feel *that* much different from your peers. Maybe none of this is true for you, but it is for me. So let's talk about me, because I'm basically egotistical. I knew that I was, well, a bit brighter than some of my fellow students (see, egotistical), although I also knew that there were people in my classes that were smarter than I was, smarter than I am still. And when I looked around the math or biology lab (where I generally studied) at one-thirty in the morning and noticed that I was one of three or four "regulars" I knew that I was perhaps putting in more effort than many. Yet it

24

never struck me as singular; I never really thought that my college experience was that much different than most. I was a good student, got A's, my teachers liked me, and I took my studies pretty seriously. I figured that most students took college pretty seriously, too.

So picture this: a rather good student, pretty sure of herself, although perhaps terrified at the moment she first stands in front of her class, attempts, yet again, to inspire her students and in turn be inspired herself. She remembers the voices of teachers before her: "I learn as much from my students, if not more, as they do from me." And she is ready to be inspired by their passion, their desire to learn, their first reading of something that she loves. She is ready to challenge them, to open their minds, to make them better students than they knew that they could be. Okay, granted, she's not sure exactly *how* she's going to do this, but she has the desire. She has been inspired by professors. Her Shakespeare professor was incredible, the woman who introduced her to Geoffrey Chaucer amazed her, even the love–hate relationship she had with the literature professor with the slow southern drawl pushed her to go to graduate school. She wants to do the same for her students. Does any of this sound at all familiar?

So she stands there, or more specifically, she sits there on the large table in the front, swinging her Birkenstock-clad feet, day after day, attempting to come up with wonderful assignments, with snappy insights, with glorious readings. She gives her students excessive time to revise, not just for the grade (in fact, some papers are never graded) but so that they can truly be proud of what they've written, can improve it and make it as close to their own visions as possible. She harps on the difference between editing and revision and yet only one student consistently and truly revises. Even those papers that are graded are seldom revised outside of what's required. She remembers back a few years, a few months even, to her own college career and her amazement at how few hours there truly are in the day. So she gives them time in class to revise, gives them *so* much feedback, suggestions, even meets one on one with her students to discuss their papers. And what does she get? In a word. . .mediocrity.

Now I must admit that the words "It's good enough" often pass my lips. I understand mediocrity. I understand just getting by; I've done it often enough myself. But I am never happy with it; I know when I'm doing it and it bothers me. Here's the difference: my students don't realize that they're just getting by. Let me clarify by way of example. On the last day of class I asked my students to write for five or ten minutes on this topic: If you were teaching this class next term what would you do differently? Most of my students were very sweet, professing that there was nothing that need be changed (darlings). But not all my students were so positive. One anonymous student told me not to expect much. In fact, I should barely expect the minimum. People assume that college students are there to work, this student continued, but in reality these "Generation Xers" don't do anything.

After I recovered from the initial shock and anger, I realized that this statement gave me some genuine insight into the mind-set of many of my students. Now don't get me wrong, I had many wonderful students, students who truly wanted to work hard and improve their writing and when they didn't do as well as they had hoped, they knew why. But, those aren't the ones that kept me up at night, questioning my teaching abilities. Yet, I also had many students who must have thought much like this one. These students don't believe that they are in college to learn; they simply want to graduate and the two are independent variables that really have little to do with each other. If this is the case then they must not expect to do well, right? Wrong (But you knew that was coming, didn't you?).

Another example, this one from my evaluations. Again, most of the students were positive and supportive, or at least ambivalent, but not all. The one student, perhaps the same one, stated that I expect too much. Another student, one that I had no idea felt this way, remarked very angrily that he had turned in all his assignments on time and had not missed more than the allowed class periods and yet I never cut him a break. He was confused as to how he could continue to get C's and D's when he never handed anything in late. Excuse me? What does that have to do with anything? Apparently, everything. You see, the two statements are related. I should barely expect the minimum from my students, I should barely expect them to turn in all their assignments on time and to show up to class, yet when I do receive this minimum amount of effort at least some of my students expect to be rewarded for it. They expect to get B's and A's, regardless of writing ability, regardless of quality. I'm sorry, but that's not how I function.

No, let me rephrase that. I'm *not* sorry. If you can't write a decent paragraph by the end of the semester then I can't pass you, and you certainly haven't earned an A or a B. I can't, I shouldn't, and I won't pass someone who can't write. It's as simple as that. My class is freshman composition, college writing, not, I repeat *not* "learn how to meet deadlines" class. . .although I'm not convinced that there shouldn't be a class like that. I digress. So I left the Graduate Office, irritated, a bit disappointed, and in a general "grumpy bear" mood (it's so easy to let one or two, let's call them less than savory evaluations, wipe out the other twenty-two). I started to obsess over next semester and how I was going to attack this problem of mediocrity.

Aye, there's the rub. Dealing with it. I suppose before I impart my infinite wisdom on how to deal with this problem we should talk a bit about why the problem exists. This is, of course, only my humble opinion and I should note that this theory owes much to hours spent, um, shall we say "conversing" in Anne Bramblett's office about teaching. It goes something like this. Once upon a time a person needed only a high school degree to get a decent job (or this is what I'm told). A college degree, boy, that was something special. Nowadays it's a bit different. A high school degree is expected and generally can't get you much of a job. This is a generalization, I'm aware, but let's just move past that. So now in order to get a decent job you've got to go to college. Today the Master's is held in much the same esteem as the college degree once was. The college degree, like the high school diploma before it, is now expected, assumed. If the college degree is expected, it seems that students who generally coasted through high school (I mean really, think back, didn't you kind of breeze through high school? Okay, except for chemistry) now believe that the same strategy is going to work for college. Everybody goes to college, right? If that's the case then everyone must graduate from college, and if everyone graduates from college then college must be a breeze, too. Ergo, college really takes no effort and you're not *really* expected to actually learn anything. If you want to learn something then go to graduate school.

Since the college degree is simply assumed, students simply assume that they will pass, and not only pass but do well. They generally have done well, and usually with minimal effort, so why not now? I'll tell you why not, because you're in my class now! Down girl. On the second day of class I explained to my students that while I thought it would be easy to pass my class it would probably be rather difficult to get an A. An A, I explained, was excellent, exceptional. One young woman raised her hand and said, "But we *can* get an A, right?" Sure. "I mean, if we revise and stuff." Wait, rewind, back up the truck. We'd better get something straight. It is absolutely possible to get an A in my class if you do excellent work. You can revise till the cows come home (Did I mention that I'm from Wisconsin?) but if you're still writing C-quality papers then you're not going to get an A. Why is this so difficult to understand?

It isn't. Here's where we get to the "but oh great and wise Alison, how do I avoid this problem?" part. First let me say, stop it, you're embarrassing me. Second, if this solution doesn't work for you, I cannot be held responsible in any way, shape, or form. Third, and this is where I impart my wisdom, make your demands very, very clear. I had a teacher in high school who had a list on the board of what he called his "Ten Demandments." It included things like "no gum" and "don't put your feet on the desk in front of you." Very clear and very effective. You should do the same. Now don't get all snippy on me; I hate people telling me what to do, too, but I'm just trying to give you some advice. It seems to me that if students, even just a handful of students, are coming into our classrooms believing that all they have to do to get an A is turn in all their assignments on time then it is our duty to quash this ugly, ugly rumor as quickly as possible. There are at least two ways to do this. One, and I think that this only works if you're teaching at a very small school, develop a reputation as a hard ass. The college I went to had a total enrollment that hovered around eight hundred. There were four or five English professors, depending on when you asked. Everyone knew everyone else and everyone knew which professors were easy and which were tough. When my younger brother (who was attending the same school at the time) was trying to decide on a literature professor he asked my advice and added, "Not Smith, I want an A." He knew that Professor Smith was tough. I'd like that reputation. But right now I teach at a big school, a state university, and a reputation is hard to come by for a TA, so I choose option two.

Option two: the syllabus. The syllabus, my friend, is where you gotta lay it all out. Let me read you a bit of my own. Ahem, "Grades. First and foremost you need to understand that turning in all assignments on time does not entitle you to an A. It does not even entitle you to pass. You will be graded on your writing ability, your revisions, your participation, and your critical thinking skills." This is just a small part of my five-page syllabus, but it sets the ground rules. It's clear, a bit harsh even, but I don't believe in sugarcoating things. I go on to detail what each grade means to me, what I expect to see in their papers, and what I expect not to see. I also read the syllabus aloud to them on the first day and have them sign a sheet stating that they read and understand everything in the syllabus. Sound elementary and ridiculous? Yeah, I agree, but I think it's necessary. Keep in mind that your requirements might be completely different from mine. It's your class, you make the rules. My point is simply that you should spell those rules out. You have to make it very clear to your students what your minimum requirements are, and stress that they are indeed the minimum.

Maybe this paints a bleak picture of students and for that I apologize, but again, I don't believe that sugarcoating does much good. Remember, the students that I'm talking about aren't the only breed. There are, of course, fabulous students. You were probably a wonderful student so you know that they exist, but those aren't the students that you need to worry about. Look, the stuff I've told you here is just what I've seen; it's just my experience. It's also only part of my experience. I love teaching. I've adored many of my students and they've brought me tremendous joy. And your experience might be completely different. As a matter of fact, at least one TA here had a truly angelic class. We're pretty sure it was a fluke of nature, but who knows? Every class is unique; you have to find a way to make your class work for you and for your students. I'm simply peddling advice here, giving you options. Just be aware that these kinds of students are out there and chances are you're going to run into them so be prepared. Don't let them shake your confidence.

Ugh, I hate endings. I feel like I should leave you with some nugget of truth, some grand idea, some solid philosophy or something to hang your teaching hat on. So here goes: just make your expectations clear. Oh, and wear comfortable shoes; it's hard to teach effectively when your feet hurt.

5

Teachable Moments

Chrissy Cooper

Teaching is an exhilarating, exhausting profession, one full of triumphs and struggles. I'm constantly amazed at how far my students come, how committed they are to learning, and how they exceed my highest expectations. That, to me, is worth everything.

The first year I taught, I felt more exhaustion and struggles than triumph and exhilaration. Most of the students' learning and affirmation of your teaching strategies doesn't come until the end of the semester. If you have a clear vision of yourself as a teacher, have clear expectations, and clear lessons, you're halfway there. The other half of teaching, however, isn't learned through teaching classes—it's passed along by practicing teachers, and it's learned on the job. Here's what I have learned along the way.

Running a Tight Ship

I have the rules, standards, and expectations written in my syllabus and then follow them. For the first third of the semester I do not make exceptions to the rules. I never make compromises on daily or weekly due dates, conference schedules, or late paper rules in the beginning of the semester. I learned you can relax the rules later, but you can never get them back if you relinquish them too early.

Excuses, Excuses

I had one semester where well over half my students were in car accidents. I finally had to tell them that I was beginning not to believe their excuses. I'm sure some of them were in accidents, but when you look at the facts, it's highly improbable that out of all the accidents in one city, most of them are happening to the people in my class. (Obviously they got wind of the fact that excuses worked on me, and they went to town with it.)

One student, missing for three weeks straight, took me aside after his final exam to show me a picture of his girlfriend who tried to kill herself one night. He had been in the hospital with her ever since.

The first thing I did was feel bad for him.

Then I felt angry because my instinct told me the theatrics were a scam.

Then I felt pressured. How do I know they were a scam? Should I look through the paper for accident reports? Will he complain or appeal if I fail him?

Then I pushed this all out of my brain for a second and figured out his grade. He had a 40 average. Now I didn't have to feel guilt or question my options. I gave him the grade he earned. I failed him. He missed class and he missed the opportunity to make arrangements to handle his absence.

Hello Out There!

It can be very difficult to get the students to participate. I just keep trying and make it an everyday event. Some classes will participate in groups, but not in class discussions. I take what I can get and build on it.

I believe a consistent classroom discussion is established by what you do or don't do on the first day of the semester. I read the syllabus with them, but I also try to have them write something and have a participation activity planned. If my students struggle to participate the first day, they struggle for the rest of the semester. If I don't get to the participation activity the first day, even if I do it the next class meeting, it's often too late, and I've noticed those semesters have yielded little participation.

If I'm doing a minilesson and soliciting participation I will wait until someone talks. I don't feel uncomfortable with their silence. I wait and wait. I rephrase the question if need be, but I wait. I don't feed them information. Someone, even if it's because they feel bad for me, will usually answer. If they still don't answer, instead of giving them the answer, I rearrange the lesson. I split them up into groups to discuss the question and to come up with a list of possible answers. I tell them they have five minutes, then ask someone in the group to write the list down, and ask someone to share it when it's time. This activity reinforces the fact that it's up to them to participate. After a few weeks, they'll get the hint that sitting there silently is not acceptable, and they'll participate more and more without having to pull teeth.

Smile

On one of my evaluations, one student said, "We should have more field trips and play more games." At first I interpreted it cynically: "Hey," I thought, "welcome to college." Then the student wrote, "She should smile more." That bothered me a little, but I thought he or she just misunderstood my Yankee stoicism. I usually come in and get to work. After all, fifty minutes goes by quickly and I have plenty to do. But then I read this: "If she hates teaching so much, why does she do it?" I was devastated. How could anyone say that? I love to teach. It's my life. I'm good at it. I give it everything.

The truth, however, was that I hated that class. Sometimes there is a strange mix of people or it's too early in the morning for everyone. Whatever the reason, I lost control of that class early on in the semester and couldn't get it back. I was shocked that *they* realized I had lost control.

After some consideration, and a whole summer break off, I went back into school in the fall smiling while I read my syllabus aloud, cracking jokes about the rules, making eye contact, and checking in with them every day by asking if they had questions about the syllabus and how their essays were developing. The turnaround was incredible. They were much more responsive, and I enjoyed teaching more. What I took to be at first immature comments, enabled me to fix my own teaching problems. I still have off days, and even off classes. Teaching, teachers, and students aren't perfect.

Grading Doesn't Have to Suck

When I was student teaching and writing narratives on students' informal papers, an English teacher walked by and said, "You shouldn't do that; they'll come to expect it." Right then and there I thought, please don't ever let me become like that teacher. Of course they'll come to expect it! They should expect feedback.

I see every time I respond to their writing as a teachable moment. I teach them even if it's just modeling spelling or complete sentences. I encourage them every time I write back. It's hard work. I do it because I'm a teacher and that's what I do: I teach every chance I get. If I think of every paper as something I have to correct, it will wear me down. If I think of every comment as a chance to teach, I'll be teaching and they'll be learning.

Don't Love Your Job to Death

If you are going to be a teacher you must keep two things in balance: give your job your all and don't give too much. A paradox? You bet. Be in control, be focused, plan, be flexible, be supportive, but then let go. Have someone you can talk to about teaching. In your first year, you may need a lot of support. Just don't forget about yourself. Take care of yourself; do whatever else you have to do in your life and with your family.

As Robert Frost said, "I am not a teacher, but an awakener." You are there to help students realize their own potential. You can awaken the intellect and creativity they already have inside them. You are the guide and the guide stays out of the way once the journey has begun.

Best Teaching Tip

When erasing the board, move the eraser up and down (not side to side) because, your, um, body will shake less.

6

Life and Breath

Kathleen Toomey Jabs

It was mid-October, the days short and cool, the trees scarlet and gold, and Melissa Hofmann was late for my section of freshman composition. Cross-country ski practice had started double sessions: weight training in the morning and aerobic activities in the afternoons. Melissa had rushed into class, not overly concerned about the time, smiling, still wearing her workout clothes: sport pants that swished as she walked and running sneakers, a tie-dyed shirt that hung almost to her knees. A baseball cap was wedged on her head, the visor tilted back just enough to show bright hazel eyes. From the back, a flaxen ponytail poked through. She lugged a navy book bag on her left shoulder and in her right hand, she cupped a plastic ventilator, an L-shaped breathing apparatus, patched at the bottom with duct tape. She brought it as a prop for the oral presentation on her research topic: cystic fibrosis. She has cystic fibrosis. She needs the "prop" to breathe.

When I called her name, Melissa slid out of her desk, stood up, nodded at some of her group mates across the circle, and held up the ventilator. "I have cystic fibrosis," she said, "and this is part of my treatment."

Melissa then told the class in a matter-of-fact voice that cystic fibrosis (CF) is the number one genetic killer for young adults and that more than 30,000 children and adults in the United States suffer from it. When she spoke her voice was slightly rasping, a trademark of CF patients, though her voice was less husky than most. She would always point out that there were patients much worse off than she.

Melissa explained how CF affects her body, how her ducts produce an abnormally thick, sticky mucus, and how she must work hard just to breathe. Later, in an essay about a friend of hers with CF, she wrote, "Sarah tested positive to a life filled with endless medications, breathing problems, digestion problems, and a disease that would eventually end her life at an early age." But Melissa did not complain. She told the class that when she was born in 1980, the life expectancy for CF patients was only sixteen years.

As Melissa described her daily treatment ritual, she put the plastic ventilator to her lips and then did mock breathing, explaining with a laugh that she couldn't haul the whole treatment vest into class because it weighed fifty pounds. The class was alert, attentive, incredulous. Melissa appeared not to notice. She was the poster child for the Cystic Fibrosis Foundation in Minnesota from 1989 to 1991, and she did a lot of public speaking then. She is not shy.

As she put down the aerosol, Melissa glibly mentioned the twenty pills a day she has to take to help with digestion, and then asked if there were any questions.

Jen asked, "Are they working on a cure?"

"Yes," Melissa said, tugging at the rim of her cap. She had collected pages of research for her report and the facts were clear in her mind. "They made a gene nine years ago. It should be a matter of time."

Rob cleared his throat, "What's the life expectancy now?"

Melissa looked down at her desk briefly. She wrapped her legs around each other. Her voice softened. "Like thirty-two or something."

Rob's face reddened. The other students glanced away, looked at their books, arranged papers.

Melissa smiled and then said, "But it'll keep going up."

I put my pen down and I noticed my chest swelled. Almost out of reflex, I inhaled deeply, tested my own lungs. I had always suspected that I would learn more from my students than they would from me and that I would take away more than I could possibly give back. Yet still, I was not prepared to witness, quite simply, the grace that comes from accepting a life you can't control and then living it. Melissa taught the class the lesson; I was honored to be the student.

2

Making Connections

Exploring Student–Teacher Relationships

On the first day of class, your students will probably be a blur of faces. But once that blur begins to separate into unique students, with unique personalities and problems, you will have to consider how to deal with these young scholars. The relationship isn't as cut and dried as you may think. "Me teacher, you student" only goes so far. The way in which we interact with students is often dependent upon our own personalities, backgrounds, and experiences. And our students react to us in particular ways because of issues in their own lives, because of their expectations about college, and their feelings about authority.

Almost all interactions with students force us into self-examination. When a student questions our authority, we question it as well. When a student confides in us about a personal problem we wonder about our qualifications, about our role in these students' lives, and about our own histories. When a student refuses to do the assignment we question our abilities. When one tells us that our class was so much fun, we wonder if that means it was too easy. When students chat amongst themselves during a lecture we get angry, but might remember doing the same thing not so many years ago. When students insinuate that we're not qualified to judge their writing, we silently wonder if they're right.

The relationship between student and teacher is, in short, complicated. For some of us, the first year of college is a recent memory, and we connect with our students because of our age, making it difficult to maintain that authoritative distance. For others, our own socioeconomic backgrounds create a backdrop for our interactions with the underdog student. Our upbringings might influence the way we deal with confrontation and discomfort. Sometimes, we are cast into the role of caretakers, a role that some of us easily embrace, stumble upon, or necessarily avoid. Add to the mix that we have the power to grade (frightening as that may be to some of us), and the relationships get even more complicated. Situations like these force us to struggle with a new understanding of ourselves and, we hope, a new understanding of our students. It's the individual relationships that we have with students that rescue us from our self-centered uncertainties, and cast us into a wider range of student and personal issues.

7

Within the Silences

Christina A. Hitchcock

Had François Rabelais been propelled into the dawn of the twenty-first century and been privileged to teach English 401 at the University of New Hampshire, he surely would have revised or negated his belief that "nature abhors a vacuum." You see, a vacuum is what you frequently have after asking your class of freshman composition students any question that requires an opinion.

I can't remember the first time it happened to me. I can't remember the third, fifth, or tenth time either. The circumstances were always the same. I would assign a brilliant, insightful, and often witty piece that I thought would provide many opportunities for lively discussion. In my mind I could envision twenty-four students talking over each other, interrupting rudely, and gesturing wildly, trying to get their points across. Alas, expectations and dreams rarely mimic reality. In the world of English 401, many well-developed questions, conceived by instructors after hours of careful thought and deliberation, fall flat on the floor in the space between instructor and students, often producing an almost audible thud, at least in the ears of the teacher. In the silence that ensues, instructors, neophytes and seasoned veterans alike, may be consumed by feelings of frustration and inadequacy. I was one of them.

I agonized over what I might be doing wrong. I seemed to have a good rapport with my students. As an older instructor, I was viewed by some of my students as the mother type and, therefore, easily approachable. As a woman with grown children and one who refuses to grow old gracefully, I pride myself for being in tune with music, movies, clothing, and overall culture of the times. I don't respond blankly to rap music references or look strangely at the blue-haired student sitting in the back of the room. It had to be something else. Maybe I needed to contextualize more. After all, I knew more about their world than they knew about mine. While some current trends may be a little weird to me, the ones I grew up with are ancient history to most of my students. Elvis Presley is not their "king," having died a number of years before any of my traditionally aged students were born; James Stuart is an icon from the

35

days of black-and-white cinema, Viet Nam is their fathers' war. That was the problem, I thought. I needed to link things together more effectively, lay a proper groundwork. Wrong. The silences continued. On the advice of another instructor, I tried letting them freewrite into a verbal answer. Nope. That wasn't going to do it. I tried a number of different strategies, but nothing worked. I longed to know the secret of the silences, and part of that secret revealed itself quite by accident.

I had assigned my class a selection of readings that included works by Jeff Foxworthy, Tim Allen, and Dennis Miller. While I will admit that these three men are more notable for their comedic talents than for their literary prowess, I chose to include them in my curriculum for several reasons, not the least of which was their recognition factor. Who among my class would not have heard of at least one of them? Who in my class would not appreciate some light reading after turning in their research essays and spending two weeks discussing the work of Charles Chesnutt and issues related to racial identity? Most importantly, though, I wanted my students to understand the power of comedy and how we, especially as writers, can often use humor to make a point that may be lost otherwise. One of the pieces was a Dennis Miller rant entitled "Power." In preparation for our discussion, I asked my students to freewrite in response to the prompt, "I have control over..."

My students usually enjoyed their freewriting time and their pens and pencils moved swiftly over the page during most of these sessions. This time, however, I sensed less activity and looked up to find pens being twirled around fingers, erasers being tapped on notebooks, and a whole array of perplexed looks. When I asked for a volunteer to read his or her freewrite, no one moved. Although I consider freewrites as private, in situations such as this one, I will ask students to reveal the basic ideas behind their writing, or name one or two things they mentioned. I approached a very popular and self-assured young woman who was looked up to for her fashion sense by her dorm-mates. She was the product of a fairly privileged background and was acclimating herself to her sorority sister status. I asked her what her first thought had been when I wrote "control" on the board. She told me that she didn't have any control. She had things to do for her sorority and for her classes; she didn't feel as though she had control over anything in her life.

As a baby boomer myself, I'd started to accept the fact that my generation is losing our collective power and influence to those generations coming after us. Most teens have more expendable income than I have, and most Gen-Xers are much more savvy than I am about e-commerce, e-trading, e-everything. Up-and-coming corporate types are driving up the price of real estate everywhere, and I can't buy a pair of shoes that don't have three-inch platforms. These kids don't just have control. They have bona fide power! Or do they? Maybe they have this power and just don't know it, or know what to do with it.

Discussion in my class that day revolved around issues of choice, control, influence, and power. At first my students were adamant that they were victimized by a system that controls all their time and dictates what they wear, what music they listen to, and how they behave. They saw themselves as victimized by expectations of others. They felt pulled in multiple directions by parental desire, peer pressure, instructors' requirements, money problems, employers, and the like. They saw themselves as being coerced and compelled by advertisers and the media. This was visually evident as they sat in my class sporting a collection of logos and labels. Status meant belonging, and status was most easily achieved by wearing the right "advertisement" on one's chest or back pocket.

In a flash, I recalled conferences with these students. One girl told me that if she didn't major in business her parents wouldn't pay her tuition. She hated business and wasn't doing well. Another student felt stressed by the expectations placed on him by parents and coaches. He was at school on an athletic scholarship and was forced to put practice before studies, but he still had to carry a certain grade point average. More than one student was in college only because everyone else they knew was in college and because their parents wouldn't allow these students to take a year off to explore. I remembered wanting to take a year off myself and my parents told me if I did so, I'd be sorry, and that I'd appreciate what they were doing for me when I was grown up. It was a mistake on their part. I ended up dropping out of school and taking much more time off than a single year.

These students, often seventeen and eighteen years old, are expected to know what they want to major in and do for the rest of their lives, but these students are not considered grown up enough to take some time off to explore their preferences and options. It made no sense to me then; it makes less sense to me now.

Parents and teachers often control every aspect of children's lives. Parents, usually meaning well, overload children with enough after-school activities to tire out three marines. While serving as the financial director of a private elementary school, I frequently saw burned-out ten year olds who would have traded everything they held dear for a few hours in front of the TV, or on the phone with friends, or just being bored. Other parents, trying to maintain upper-middle-class lifestyles, or holding their families together on working poor salaries, saddle children with adult responsibilities without teaching them how or allowing them to make adult choices. For all their honors and accolades, so many college-age students feel accomplished and powerless at the same time.

And there are the teachers who allow students to learn and grow, as long as these students respond according to certain scripts. Secondary school teachers often employ the "my way or no way" method of teaching. Students who have been penalized for writing subjective papers are nearly paralyzed when they have to write a paper with the word "I" in it. Objectivity in writing often serves to distance the writer from the writing, and makes it easy for the writer to appropriate the views and thoughts of others, often views and thoughts that the teachers feel are the correct ones. As a result of these experiences, students sometimes offer little feedback in class because they don't know what their college instructors want to hear. One student asked me what I wanted her to learn from a certain reading. I told her I wanted her to think, consider, respond, and react. She looked at me so strangely that I was tempted to check the bathroom mirror to see if my clothes were inside out.

But where does this fit in with writing? And what does this have to do with the silences in the classroom? Opinions are closely related to choices. Just as students are not valued for their (often unique) opinions, they are rarely given true choices to make in high school classes. The assignment to write a report on a book of your choice often comes with a list of preapproved books from which to choose. Students select topics and then teachers shoot them down. Part of this response comes from the legal issues that prohibit the incorporation of certain subjects into the public classroom or the ideologies upon which some private schools are founded. Administrations and parents often have their own ideas of what their children should think and learn. In fairness to teachers, sometimes they, themselves, have few choices.

I do understand the role of rules and limitations in schools, even if I sometimes think they go way too far. The problem is that often a student has no transition period between the closely controlled environment of home and high school and the fairly free environment of college, especially when that college is a rather large public university. Three months is not enough time to shed the learned constraints and become free-thinking, independent adults. As instructors, we need to realize that the self-assured self-presentations of these students in our classrooms are often careful constructs that mask deep insecurities.

Knowing this makes it easier for instructors to understand the deer in the headlights look many students have when told that they can write their research essay on any topic they choose. Finally, I have a better idea why it takes my students longer to select their research essay questions than it does to research, prewrite, write, and revise the essays. And bear in mind that revisions are problematic for the same reasons I have mentioned. In many high school English courses, there is one way and one way only to do something. They are expected to rewrite to correct, not change. Revision as re-vision is an alien concept to these students. I now equate revising an essay with furnishing a room. That metaphor has made the idea of changing things to make them different, to view them from a different angle, a little easier for my students to understand.

During that first semester, our classroom discussion of power continued during the remaining weeks and occurred within the context of whatever we had read. We talked about manipulation and persuasion, and I continued to point out those places where they had made choices, exercised their power, influenced others, or taken control of a situation. They quickly opened up. So during each semester that has passed since the first one, I have tried to add one more way to provide my students with power over their lives, at least within the context of English 401. I started with my introduction to the course. My opening remarks on the first day of class now include three very important statements. I tell my students that I want them to find the "I" in "writer." I also inform them that I want them to learn about themselves through their own writing and the writing of others. To that end, I employ the memoir, as both reading task and writing product, quite extensively. Most importantly, I stress that I want them to expand, and grow, and take chances and I assure them that experimentation carries no penalties. I'm sincere, but I can see that they have a hard time buying into what I'm telling them.

I have added writing assignments that require students to discover who they are and render opinions. One of those assignments is an essay in which each student must discuss her own philosophy of life and its genesis. Another assignment is to find a newspaper article and disagree with it in a letter to the editor. I've made portfolio requirements as loose as possible while still requiring a portfolio. Students get to choose what they want me to grade for the semester; they are free to throw out assignments on which they feel they have done poorly, and they are encouraged to interpret these assignments in the broadest possible sense. Of course, I still get lots of questions asking me if it's alright to do this or that. I just keep reassuring them that it is.

And the silences? I believe that no matter what I do, the silences will creep in and remind me that my better understanding of the problem does not solve it. Now when the silences emerge, I just tell my students to grab their notebooks and write down whatever they are thinking. Maybe they are reluctant to share, but that's fine with me. They are thinking, and for that purpose, silences can be very productive.

8

The Personal Is Pedagogical

Joseph P. Montibello, Jr.

While I try to avoid repeating the same phrases over and over to my freshman writing class, there is one phrase I seem to return to always: "Whatever you write, it should be something only you could have written." The "process" approach to teaching, with its emphasis on individual students finding their own ways into writing, makes it necessary for students to write from their own subjective position, whether they are writing personal essays or research papers. The power of the process method (when it works) is that each student can use his or her own strengths and talents to improve him- or herself. The underlying assumption is that students with different skills will learn better, and ultimately write better, in different ways.

So how does this apply to their teachers?

We are just as diverse a group. We vary widely in age, backgrounds, strengths, and weaknesses. We vary in interests—some of us are dedicated to teaching writing as a career and profession, others are graduate students who have different goals but need (or want) to teach on a short-term basis. We each have our own subject position that we bring to the classroom every day, and we teach from that position whether we are conscious of it or not. Just as we ask students to be aware of themselves, shouldn't we spend some energy looking into our backgrounds? The personal is pedagogical whether we like it or not.

For me, looking at the personal means facing the fact that I am an adult child of an alcoholic. My mother drinks, heavily; she has for as long as I can remember, and I know that she first started drinking well before she became pregnant with me (at age nineteen). Growing up in a household that was run by an alcoholic was an erratic, unsettling affair, and while my mother was not terribly violent, there was the constant sense that at any moment she could be suddenly set off. I learned very early how to read the air when I walked into my house, to listen carefully to my mother's voice for the edge that would tell me that today might be a good day to stay outside. I developed the habit of simply going along to get along, hearing what people wanted and giving it to them, and generally not rocking the boat.

Now I am married and living away from my family. It was not until I moved out of my mother's house that I gained enough distance from the situation to admit to myself that my mother's behavior had affected me. I've always believed (wanted to believe?) that I did whatever I wanted, that my behavior was the realization of my own will. But thinking about the constructedness of a subject position a student takes made me think about how I am constructed, as well as constructing myself, as a teacher.

I have found that I am fairly lax about the way the class runs—students showing up a little late or talking among themselves unobtrusively during discussions seem to know that their actions carry no consequences. I often feel that I am able to teach only because students "let" me; I am relying on their previous conditioning and politeness to keep the class in order. As a child of an alcoholic, it goes against my experience to insist on my own authority or to demand that others follow certain rules. (An alcoholic's behavior is notoriously unpredictable—I often felt that while my mother set many rules for me, there was no set of rules that governed her actions.) So I say nothing, or make an indirect and half-joking comment, and the behavior I object to disappears for awhile. I grew up feeling that anything I said or did could be suddenly and unexpectedly called into question. As a teacher, I hold a position of some authority. But I have a tendency to react to some situations in the classroom as if I were an equal or subordinate person. While my pedagogy demands that I empower my students rather than emphasize the unequal power relations we have, I also have a responsibility to keep some order and make sure that I treat my students fairly. Like it or not, I am an institutional insider compared to my freshmen students. When I revert to the role of the powerless child, who can joke but never take control, I tend to let some students miss deadlines or bend the rules—and usually this process favors the more aggressive students who are willing to push. Many students can sense my "go along to get along" attitude and know immediately that they can take advantage of it.

One example of this occurred when a student came to me after class. She told me that she wasn't going to have time over the next two days to complete her final draft of a paper that was due because of a "huge test" coming up in another class. I told her that she probably should have worked on the paper earlier if she had known that this was coming up, but she reminded me that I had told the class of the final due date only recently, and that the test she was taking had cropped up in similar fashion. She told me she felt bad asking but wanted to do a good job on her essay and didn't feel that she would be able to if she handed it in on the day I assigned. I told her that it wouldn't be a problem.

Immediately after she left, I felt that I was wrong—she had known that we were working on that paper even before she had known the due date. If everyone in the class knew that all you had to do was tell the teacher that you had some other important thing to do, to get out of doing work, class would be in shambles.

But I didn't want to hurt her feelings. She sounded really sincere about wanting to do a good job on the paper. I felt guilty that I had waited until the last minute to let the students know about the due date (although I had told them about a week ahead and they had already produced one draft of the paper). I thought that it would be better for her to spend time and do a good revision than for me to "teach her a lesson" about being responsible (by now I was beginning to rationalize excuses for the young woman that she hadn't even thought of). And the writing really was what the class was all about, right? I felt bad about it but accepted her late paper without further comment and without marking off on her grade.

The pedagogy that I believe in focuses on the students—what do they need to get out of my class, how can I present materials in stimulating ways, how can I use what they already know to get them to move forward and improve their writing? By taking the "sage off the stage," by being human and presenting myself as someone who is still learning about writing, I can connect with my students and gain a level of comfort with them. Unfortunately, this method of teaching also makes it easy for me to slip into an ineffectual mode of worrying too much about what students think of me and of the class.

Things like this happen from time to time—I run out of things to say toward the end of class and ask students to discuss things a bit, but they are already packing up and moving on. "It's only a couple of minutes," I think. A student misses a conference, so I reschedule it for another time, telling him not to worry about it when he apologizes. I set up an atmosphere where students who want to follow the rules are welcome to, and those who don't needn't really worry—as long as they (eventually) do their work, I'm not going to bother them too much.

I'm glad to say that I have a strong rapport with my class. We do have fun from time to time, and I feel that most of them have been progressing in their writing. I just wonder if things might not run better if I was a bit more efficient, a bit more authoritative, a bit more willing to rock the boat when necessary. I don't want students to take me too seriously—I'm not the great expert from whom their knowledge shall flow—but maybe if I were more assertive on those little things, they wouldn't feel inclined (as I sometimes think they are) to do the least amount possible that will get them by. I am working on trying to insist on things, getting students to work harder, and my enthusiasm about the class seems to help (sometimes). The problem isn't students undercutting my authority, but me doing it myself. I still try to appease everyone—not just my mother (who is still unpredictable but no longer runs my life) but also others who have given me no reason to feel that they will treat me as my mother once did. Most of my students have been very friendly and respectful, yet somehow when I stand in front of my class, I can feel like a little boy standing in front of twenty-five alcoholic parents. To teach more effectively, I must recognize the power dynamic in my classroom as it really is.

9

It's Not What You Signed Up For

Zen and the Art of Teaching Freshman English

Olga Lambert

I was a psychology major in college, and many of my classes emphasized the value of getting one's thoughts and feelings down on paper. So I was not really surprised that writing about my fears, doubts, and disappointments felt liberating. However, I did not quite expect it to have the same effect on my students. Maybe it was because on the first day of class, almost all of them talked about how much they hated English and what a waste of time writing was. In any case, I was completely unprepared for what happened on the third day of class. As students were reading their personal-experience essays aloud to each other, I wrote in my teaching journal:

> These guys are laughing. Good. I'm constantly taking the pulse of this class. The two dudes who aren't reading are chewing and fidgeting. They look pretty shy, actually. I have to remember that they are afraid of sounding dumb, of revealing too much of themselves, of people not liking them. Just like me. I can't believe how young I am sometimes. Unfortunately. All the groups with the exception of the reluctant dudes sound loud and lively. Good. I *am* totally taking the pulse of this class. But what am I supposed to do? How am I supposed to know? God, I hope Kate is not crying. Her voice is quivering. She *is* crying. I feel guilty. I was supposed to do this, right?

Earlier that day, I had my first conference with Kate, and we went over the rough draft of her paper. The experience she wrote about was still painfully fresh in her mind—only three weeks earlier, Kate's parents had told her and her brother that they were getting a divorce. Kate, who had always thought that she had a "perfect" family, was crushed. As I read her paper, she talked about how angry she was at her parents, but her eyes were dry. Now, however, she was bawling, and I was convinced that it was all my fault. Why did I have to make her talk about something so painful in front of two strangers? What if she was deeply traumatized by this? Of course, I was only doing what the more experienced teachers told me to do, and she could have chosen to write about summer camp instead, right?

I got up and walked over to Kate. "Are you alright?" I asked guiltily. To my amazement, she smiled. "Yeah," she said, sniffling, "I'm okay." Her workshop partners were trying to comfort her. I felt like a therapy group facilitator.

As I soon discovered, freshman English *was* therapy. In their papers, my students struggled with difficult and often painful issues, and I was overwhelmed by the sheer amount of adversity these eighteen-year-olds had been through. Jamie wrote her first essay about her best friend's drinking, which I thought was a serious enough problem. In conference, however, she said that she regretted not having enough courage to write about what *really* mattered to her. Her next paper detailed a two-year high school relationship in which her boyfriend repeatedly hit and raped her. Once, after class, another student asked to speak to me in my office. He explained that the reason he was so often absent during the previous two weeks was that his sister had overdosed on heroin and he was taking care of her. I was not surprised—from Jeff's writing and our conferences, I knew about his sister's drug use, their parents' divorce, and Jeff's troubles with the law. I hoped, however, that writing and talking would help him cope with all that.

Apparently, it did, because in his course evaluation at the end of the semester, Jeff wrote that he would continue to use freewriting as a way of dealing with stress. I was proud.

> A lot of people are mentioning anxiety and not liking themselves or the way they look. That I can (or definitely could) relate to. These guys are all really interesting. And they seem to get along with each other. Jess said that they are not going to get anywhere if she keeps talking. Funny. Jeff says enough man-bashing. No kidding. It's an interesting group—Jess, Meghan, and Jeff— but they seem to be having fun. Jess said that she admires her parents because they're still together. I admire mine for the same reason. How normal, idealis- tic, and even naive they seem underneath their cynical facades. I just wish they would drop them when they're here; after all, I am barely older than they are. Sometimes I want them to forget that, but sometimes the age thing comes in really handy. They talk about mean people, depression, divorce, their families.

Most books for composition teachers talk about a "community of writers"—a place where students feel safe sharing their writing with each other and where they work together to help each person express him- or herself on paper as effectively as possible. While I have certainly seen the glimpses of that utopia in my classroom, at least half the time my students and I were not even close. Many times, when they answered my questions about the reading in monosyllables or rushed through a revision workshop hoping to get out of class early, I was convinced that I just did not have what it takes. Sometimes I was sure that they knew I was a fraud; I felt scrutinized and ill at ease. Of course,

I never would have admitted it to another TA or, God forbid, any of my professors. I "absolutely loved teaching" all the time, each of my class sessions was "wonderful," and my students were always "very insightful and enthusiastic."

As it turned out, during that first semester I learned much more than how to grade papers and choose reading assignments. As my students tried to come to terms with who they were by writing about their experiences, I started to realize that doing my best was always enough—that perfection was both unattainable and unnecessary. I also discovered that "counseling" was a much bigger part of my job than I could have anticipated. Before I started teaching, I had heard from more experienced instructors that because freshman composition is a much smaller class than most freshman courses, students often feel comfortable enough to share personal problems with each other and the teacher. I was told to be a good listener and if the issues my students talked about were serious, refer them to Counseling Services. To be honest, I was even excited about trying out the skills I had learned in my college psychology classes, but I never thought I would have to do it more than once or twice a semester.

I was wrong. Almost every week, usually in conference, one of my students would mention a difficult romantic relationship, a friend's eating disorder, or a family problem. Their papers were full of even more disturbing experiences—serious car accidents, legal troubles, sexual abuse. Sometimes I found myself afraid to say the wrong thing and make a student feel worse—I remembered the few occasions when I had confided in a professor only to be stung with a tactless or dismissive remark. Occasionally, I would replay a conversation over and over in my mind, analyzing everything I said and hoping that I had not been insensitive.

Gradually, I realized that most students who shared their problems with me were just glad that someone was listening to them, someone who seemed interested in what they had to say and did not tell them that they were overreacting or that the situation was their fault. Besides, writing usually provided my students with all the insights I could not give them. I did have to contact Counseling Services once—I was concerned about one of my students who seemed severely depressed—but most of the time, listening was enough.

I also found that being young, which I saw as a handicap at first, actually helped me relate to my students. After all, I had struggled with many of the same issues only four years earlier, and I remembered that time very well. Sometimes, if I had an experience similar to the one a student was talking about, I would mention it. When you are eighteen and something unfortunate happens to you, it is often easy to believe that you are the only person in the world to have ever been in this predicament.

Some people may tell me that it is not a college instructor's job to listen to students' personal problems and be concerned about their self-esteem. However, I firmly believe that most of the learning that takes place in college happens outside the classroom, and that includes learning to cope with life's difficulties by talking and writing about them. I keep that in mind when I walk into the classroom. I also remind myself that some students will not seek professional help for their problems because of the stigma that is still attached to "seeing a shrink" and that talking to a writing instructor does not threaten to damage anyone's pride. Last but not least, I remember what being eighteen feels like.

10

Boundaries of Caring

Nancy Eichhorn

Heather sits in my office, mascara-tinged tears staining her white T-shirt. She rubs her eyes, continues reading her personal essay: 'Randy Gomez died today,' my mom said quietly as if it took all her energy to say the words. My body felt weak, and my knees buckled as I fell to the ground. A single tear dripped onto the floor. . . ."

I look as if I am listening, but Heather's words take me back twenty-one years to the intersection of Alta Arden and Howe Avenue. I'm clutching a piece of black plastic, a shattered section of Michael's motorcycle helmet. The California Highway Patrolman won't let me cross the street, won't let me near the paramedics. I'm told to meet them at Kaiser Hospital.

My fiancé died that night. My life, at age nineteen, forever twisted by alcohol, and Michael's need to speed, to prove his virility. I know the pain, loss, confusion Heather feels. I know the feelings of anger and injustice. Do I share my story? Does she need to know that I can truly sympathize?

I offer a hug as she falters. Randy died two days earlier. It's too soon to be writing this, but it helps Heather deal with the shock, the disbelief. Writing is therapeutic, cathartic. Heather will write on this topic for years, whether for public display or personal journaling. It will help her accept reality.

But does she need to hear my story to understand her own? How far do I go to support her emotional needs?

At the University of New Hampshire, freshmen, like Heather, are required to take English 401. The main emphasis is essay writing, which often includes personal essays, and students, many experiencing personal essay writing for the first time, often reveal their innermost pain—suicide, accidental death, eating disorders, sexual assaults, parental abuse, and homesickness. Biweekly conferences allow time for teachers and students to discuss the essays and to connect. Veteran teachers agree that students cherish the conference time. And most of the time, the talk centers on writing, on stylistic decisions the student made.

But occasionally, the content comes to the forefront. As teachers we must decide when to share our personal lives and how much. And, we must know what our responsibilities are in terms of responding to students' needs.

John is at the university on a football scholarship. He's away from home for the first time, away from his girlfriend, Dawn. The transition is difficult, even more so because his relationship isn't secure. He writes of the night he cheated on Dawn and the ensuing struggle to remain close, especially now that he's forty-five minutes away. He needs a scene to show the intimacy they shared before the fateful night but isn't quite clear. I think a moment and say, "If I were to create a scene showing intimacy it would be about the night I had emergency surgery. After the anesthesiologist finished my injection, I passed out holding Paul's right hand. I woke up an hour later holding Paul's right hand. Whether we're walking, shopping, watching TV, driving, Paul and I hold hands. We can even be fighting, and we're holding hands."

John smiles with recognition. He understands. Then he asks, "Is Paul your husband, boyfriend?"

I'm silent. My first reaction is to kick myself, and then I think, why did I use my life as an example? Why didn't I refer John to an essay in our class reader? I had promised myself I wouldn't share details of my personal life, but it comes so naturally when talking about personal essays. I connect with students' stories, and I share authentic reactions. But now I'm stuck.

Do I tell John that Paul and I were to be married last month but the wedding was called off? Do I tell him it was one of the worst summers of my life, that Paul and I are struggling, that the diamond ring on my right hand belongs on my left?"

I take a deep breath and say, "Paul is my fiancé," and leave it at that.

I've worked hard to maintain professional distance. Simple acts like using the school email system not my personal account, offering the English department phone number not my home number, and referring to students as "the" students not "my" students keep distance. The word distance may offend people, but I'm not suggesting that teachers don't care. Part of why we entered the profession is because we do care and instinctually want to help other people. What I am saying is that we need perspective to ensure that we don't become overly involved, even when a student is sitting directly in front of us, tears welling up in her eyes, spilling over onto her cheeks. It's hard to stop short of taking care of, but I think this is the ultimate difference. It's okay to care about a student, but it's not my role to take care of him or her, even if students expect more.

> There are some teachers that are only that—teachers. They are like machines. There are others that become people to their students. Those teachers share their lives with their students, and they really want to get to know their students beyond who they are in the classroom.

Samantha wrote this in her first class essay about a significant moment. A high school teacher extended herself beyond the classroom and included students in her personal life. Because this woman shared stories about her boyfriend, about her family, her own frustrations, she was deemed a good teacher—she cared about her students. I flinched when I read Samantha's essay because I struggle with this boundary to care. There was a time I cared too much. I tried to take care of a student and the end result was disastrous.

I first met Chris a few years ago while I was teaching a high school reading/writing class. He sauntered into my classroom almost a month after the semester had started. His hair brushed the tops of his lean shoulders, his left eye was hidden under a mass of bangs. He wore army fatigues and steel-toed black boots. Dog tags dangled, clanked as he stepped into the room. His walk was an art form: knees bent, body slouched back over his heels, back erect, each stride a concentrated placement of heel to toe. He reeked of stale cigarette smoke with a hint of marijuana.

He refused to make eye contact. Pretty difficult considering the eight of us sat around one rectangular table. After two weeks, I introduced Chris to Anne Rice's trilogy about vampires. Chris identified with the main character Lestat—the vampire's total disregard for social conformity, his egomaniacal demonstrations, his flagrant behaviors, intrigued Chris. From shared writings, I knew Chris wanted to be free of a tyrannical father, of a neglectful mother.

After years of bitter fighting, Chris's parents had finally divorced. Chris lived with his mother. He overdosed on narcotics. Paramedics pumped his stomach, and his mother shipped him to his father, a lifetime military man. His dad commuted to work at 0600 each day. Chris was roused, groomed, and fed before Dad left him with strict instructions detailing chores and responsibilities. Chris was left to his own devices until he chose to arrive, if he chose to arrive, at school at 0710.

After a month in class, Chris read and wrote stories and poems more sophisticated than his junior year status indicated. But his personal journal entries reflected desperation and isolation. My written responses always included the same information: Chris, if you need to talk with someone, the school counselor is down one flight of stairs; Chris, if you write about suicide or self-mutilation (he often arrived at school with surface-level slashes across his wrists), I am required by law to tell the counselor.

But I didn't like the counselor assigned to my students. She had attended my class for a while, "to bond with the kids outside of the group therapy room," until she stated in class that she hated to write so she understood why my students hated to write, too. I felt she was out of line. She felt she was right in line. She stayed downstairs from then on. But I knew I didn't have the training to deal with Chris' emotional issues. I wanted to do the right thing so I suggested that Chris contact her. Chris chose to confide in me.

Chris needed emotional support. But was that my role?

The director of Special Education Services had hired me knowing I had no previous experience teaching high school or special education. My background included six years of elementary education in California before moving to New

Hampshire to earn my master's degree in education as a reading specialist at the University of New Hampshire. The students in the class were dual coded in the special education system. They had to be both learning disabled and emotionally challenged to enter the experimental reading and writing program I designed and taught. I became a special education caseworker, a role I was not trained to fulfill. I was responsible for the students' educational program, support services, and extensive paperwork mandated by state and federal guidelines for special education.

Sitting in my office at the University of New Hampshire, with a second master's degree in nonfiction writing, I know I am qualified to teach freshman composition, but I face the familiar conflict of caring as I read anonymous midterm evaluations from my students:

> I think that the conferences with you every other week are one of the best parts of this class. It gives each of us a chance to speak with you one to one, which helps us know you on a more personal level. Most college courses you barely get to know the teacher.

Another says:

> The conferences are great. Getting the one-on-one attention with specific problems that I sometimes have. It's also a great way for professor Eichhorn to get to know me and a way for myself to become more familiar with her. The whole idea of conferences made the transition to college a lot easier, and made me feel more comfortable because I know where I could go if I have any problem.

While their words sound positive, my intuition is in a tightly wound knot. I am a teacher and it's my job to care. But how much?

Students come to college filled with expectations. Unfortunately, many students are quickly overwhelmed. Their "top ten percent of the class" status is now commonplace. Support systems, whether family, friends, ministers, pastors, rabbis, or special teachers, are left behind. They're on their own to make new friends, to find a place to fit in. General education classes are large—fifty or more students sit in lecture halls. Professors, who can't know all their students' names, rely on TAs to run smaller lab or discussion sections. Freshmen can feel lost, until they take freshman English—the teacher knows their name, notices when their seat is empty, listens to their stories and cares.

Samantha's topic for her required research essay is eating disorders. She isn't sure just what angle she wants to take—anorexia, bulimia, compulsive overeating. She's interested because her mom recently started overeating, and Samantha wants to find out why. We talk about a focus and quietly Samantha says, "Well, when I first got here, I went overboard at meals. I walked into the dining hall and thought, hmmm, I'll have a little of this and some of that, and oh, pasta, I'll have some of that. I was overeating every meal." She points to her body implying that she's gained weight.

Eating disorders run rampant on college campuses, and students will write about their battles with food as if it's an alien creature that consumes their desires, drags them down. Thomas Newkirk, director of composition studies at UNH, teaches my English 910 class: teaching college composition. He uses essays in our class to stimulate conversations about body perception issues, about food in society. He provides examples for us to use in our classes. But do I want to go there? Do I want to invite conversations about eating disorders?

I listen to Samantha ponder her research, and I wonder: Do I tell her I've done extensive research on bulimia and have an article being published in an alternative health magazine? Do I tell her it's a first-person account based on experiences that happened twenty years ago? Or do I share my compassion simply by saying I understand your dilemma and recommend an appointment at the student-counseling center?

I know my beliefs, experiences, and background knowledge influence my responses. We all react from our past, but I've learned that my issues cannot come to the forefront. For my emotional safety and well-being, I need to maintain healthy boundaries. One of the major causes of teacher burnout is from caring too much, from taking responsibility in areas where we have no control.

Chris left a note with a cassette tape on my desk at school. He told me not to feel bad and thanked me for caring when no one else did. He had recorded songs by groups with names like Poison and Primus Pig as well as singer/songwriter Tori Amos to tell his tale. Earlier in the semester, Chris had handed me a blank tape on which to share my emotional state of mind. He asked me to respond by making a tape of my own. I did. I shouldn't have. I crossed the line between teacher and individual, between professional life and private life.

When I began my tape, I recorded upbeat songs by the Pointer Sisters, the Doobie Brothers, Cecilio and Kapono. But it felt false. It wasn't me. It was the public image I wanted to portray. Besides, I knew Chris was savvy, and my veil of happiness was thin. Chris wanted truth, authenticity. I wanted to take care of Chris, to make his pain go away. I believed that if I shared my feelings and my coping strategies Chris would see that all people cope with pain, loss, and suffering. That it's human nature to feel, but then you let the feelings pass and you move ahead. It was easy to think. It was easy to believe Chris would understand.

So I recorded songs by Led Zeppelin and Tori Amos to share my sadness, my sense of isolation after leaving my friends and family in California three years earlier, my inability to voice my emotions. At age thirty-four, I didn't share my feelings easily. I taped a song by the Marshall Tucker Band about finding places to run to, places to go and die to express my frustration with life.

I was absent the day Chris left his note. His father called me at home asking if I had heard from Chris. He hadn't checked in after school; his father had reason to be concerned. I had eight students that year, including Chris. He was enrolled in my class because of his academic profile—a withdrawn, habitual truant. There was a notation of an attempted suicide and *Beware of the father* was written in red ink. I never knew who wrote those comments.

Chris was missing for two days. I sleuthed clues from his tape, from previous notebook entries in our readers/writers notebooks, which we used in class to respond to literature, to our writing, and to one another. I searched all the beaches in New Hampshire. There are only eighteen miles of coastline but lots of tiny beaches along the way. I scoured York Beach, Wells Beach, and Ogunquit Beach in Maine. I wandered through cemeteries in New Castle, Portsmouth, Hampton, and Rye. Nothing.

I felt driven to find him. When he left his note on my desk, he had left me in charge. He had put his life in my hands. It felt like a test. How often did I really listen? How well did I really know him? How much did I really care?

While my experience with Chris might be considered unusual, the feelings, the reactions, the human desire to connect and to protect are real no matter where you teach, no matter what age you teach. College students are no different. They deal with abusive parents and partners, date rapes, and sexual harassment. They face challenges that no one is emotionally ready for, but at eighteen years of age, college freshmen face these situations alone. For many, it's the first time living on their own. The structure of the English 401 class—twenty-four students maximum with required conferences—encourages personal relationships. Most students reach out and hold on. It's up to us, as their teachers, to know how to access available resources such as phone numbers for the counseling center, for the Sexual Harassment and Rape Prevention hot line, and for Planned Parenthood. No, it is not our role to act as counselors, but we need to offer some guidance when a student is in crisis. Students do commit suicide. Students are raped. Students come to class wearing heavy layers of foundation to hide a black eye—the result of an angry boyfriend's attack.

Lee arrives ten minutes late to our conference, out of breath from climbing the three flights of stairs; the smell of stale cigarette smoke follows him into the room. He has the second draft of his personal essay in hand.

Lee is dealing with his cousin's recent suicide and a friend's overdose. He shares that his way of dealing is not to deal. His father doesn't share feelings. His grandfather didn't either. His mother, turning to Lee for support, wonders why her son remains disconnected. Lee is struggling to maintain distance, but he's drowning. Dark circles under his eyes are shadows of intense grief and loneliness. He writes about his drug and alcohol issues, claims he's moving away from their grasp. But he adds that he isn't perfect. Pain breaks through as he writes in his essay, "When is someone going to care about me, take care of me?"

What am I supposed to do? Do I worry that Lee might be suicidal? That he might get so drunk or high one night that he doesn't care about life anymore? Or do I treat his essay as a piece of writing and talk about setting a scene, letting the details tell the story?

Looking for clues about Chris's whereabouts, I opened his school locker and I knew. Taped inside was a travel story I had written for the local newspaper about my adventures exploring a small tourist resort, about a one-hour ferry ride from the Rhode Island mainland. I called the police to say that a runaway might be on their island, that he was most likely on the beach just beyond the historic lighthouse, and that this seventeen-year-old planned to commit suicide.

The local constable found Chris on the beach drenched with rain, drunk, stoned on acid, bleeding from slashes across both wrists.

Two months later, I met Chris at the public library. A pile of books were on the table in front of him: *Interview with a Vampire*, by Anne Rice; a book by Jack Kerouac detailing his drug-induced journeys; a poetry book entitled *Reflections on a Gift of Watermelon Pickle* that I had bought months ago when Chris started writing narrative poems. My gift to a dedicated writer.

Chris had spent the past two months at a psychiatric facility. I was hired to tutor him, to play academic catch-up so he could reenter his classes and finish his junior year.

Chris sat in a library chair, legs crossed at the knee. Black Army boots, shined to regulation standards, reflected fluorescent light. His left leg ticked. It always did—at least since I'd known him. Six-inch-wide white bandages covered the insides of his wrists. We went outside so he could smoke.

Chris inhaled. A long, slow, deliberate draw on an unfiltered Camel cigarette. He exhaled and talked about his time in therapy. He said he mentioned his father, his mother, and his older sister, who also tried to commit suicide several times while she lived at home. But he listened far more than he shared during group therapy sessions. That didn't surprise me. As long as I'd known him, he'd avoided counselors.

Chris tried to engage me, privately, emotionally. He didn't care about the biological structure of DNA, the current biology class curriculum. He wanted to know what I was feeling. I refused to divulge that information.

He asked me how I was. I told him that I was fine. He pressed. He gazed into my eyes, direct eye contact, waited for a response that wasn't coming. I refused to tell Chris I wanted to leave the school, that it was too intense dealing with the emotional needs of my students. Chris' needs weren't the only ones, they all needed me. I felt drained. I felt like a failure. I had let Chris down. I wondered who else I would fail.

I asked him why he did it; he told me that it was because of me.

Part of me knew his accusation was intentional, that he was lashing out to hurt me. But another part of me also knew I had crossed the line when I gave Chris my tape. There's a line that teachers don't cross between professional relationships and personal. I blurred that boundary. My intentions were sincere, genuine, caring. I never meant to hurt this child. My god, I never meant to hurt any child.

Balancing the head and heart makes the teaching profession tremendously challenging. Every day, as I listen to students, I think before responding. And

I limit how much of my life I share. Where I used to reach out to take care of, I now stand back and work to empower students to make their own decisions, to take control of their lives.

Shelia's dressed in sweats, just in from the horse barns. She gathers her composure and begins reading her essay about meeting her lover for the first time. Her face reddens. A smile appears as she shifts her body in the chair. There's a certain smile a woman gets when talking about the man she loves—there's an energy that radiates. I say, "I know that smile." Then ask her, "I'm curious about the initial moment when you two connected. Can you tell me more?"

11

Becoming a Witness

Andrew Lopenzina

I began my career as a teacher with the typical anxieties that I would somehow fall flat on my face, that my students would disrespect me, and my best efforts to be inspirational, to make students really want to write, would be woefully inadequate. I didn't really believe these things, however. They were simply anxieties. They lurked in the corners of my mind in the weeks leading up to my first class, and they made an all out assault on my psyche in the final days before I actually started teaching.

But simultaneously, even up to the last minute before entering the classroom (as I paced the floor of my office in a mild panic, repeatedly checking my watch, going over in my mind the first few things I thought I might say to my students), I thought that I would be good. I thought I would be very good. I had mapped out a trajectory for my semester, aligned the readings to the various steps I hoped to make on my imagined arc towards turning unmolded inarticulate freshman into reading/writing machines, and saw how I would gradually nurture their appreciation for the process. In other words, I thought I would be a success.

But still I paced in my office, dreading failure.

I think every endeavor of this sort should be met with an equal mix of terror and heightened expectations. The fact is, I have rarely known a success in my life that wasn't somehow tinged with the specter of failure. There are always niggling little doubts that maybe you didn't do as well as you might have, or the fear that any given success was somehow a fluke and could never be repeated. I am especially prone to this sort of self-conscious back-stabbing and my first semester of teaching was characterized by an ever-shifting sense of my level of achievement.

If there was one student in my class who best helped me characterize the mixed sense of accomplishment and failure I was destined to feel, it was Sam. I remember facing my class on that first morning. They were all sitting there quietly in the dark when I came in, hands folded on tops of desks, nobody talking. I attempted to turn on the lights as I entered the room, but the switch was on some kind of automated delay that proved too technologically daunting for me to master in that one interminable moment of making my entrance. I kept flicking the switch up and down to no effect. My first failure, and I hadn't even made it to my desk yet. I taught that first class assisted only by the gloam of natural light that came in through the windows.

After briefly introducing myself and stumbling through the syllabus with them, I handed out index cards and had the students write down some bare basic facts about their lives. Then we went around the room, introducing ourselves to one another, reading from what we'd written on our index cards, or, more often, paraphrasing what had been written. I was immediately struck by how respectful they all were, well spoken, clean cut, all white. Is it only the state of New Hampshire that churns out such students? On the one hand, I was relieved. It seemed as though their previous institutional conditioning had smoothed all the rough edges out for me. I would actually have to exhort them, in later classes, to occasionally curse in their papers, admit to lapses in judgment, confess that they had ever smoked, opened a beer, thought subversive thoughts, actually lived. But I was also disappointed. Wasn't there one rebel in the lot? Wasn't there a student that might reflect some of my own institutional misgivings as a youth?

Around the room it went, each student telling a little of their history. There were students who had spent their summers as camp counselors, some who had worked in convenience stores, one who was passionate about surfing of all things (he was from Jersey), others who were into music and sports. Sam's short narrative was a little different. I could tell right away that he had a little more edge to him. Throughout the first week of classes, he had a tendency to merge in my mind with the other three or four tall, athletic-looking youths in baseball caps who sat with their desks against the back wall facing me. Still, whenever he spoke I was always forced to look twice. Alone of all my students, he carried the ring of challenge in his voice. There was something in his tone that called me out, but not in any way I could put my finger on.

On that first day, he announced to the class that his name was Sam, and that he'd always been a bit of a loose cannon. He didn't say it quite that way. But he told us how he'd always done things his own way, and had gotten into trouble for it. He said, as a child, they used to call him "one-way Sam," because everywhere they went as a family, they'd be going one way and he'd be going the other. But he said he'd had to change his attitude over the previous summer. His father had been diagnosed with kidney cancer, and Sam had to spend his first summer after high school graduation working two jobs to help support his family. He said he felt determined to do well in college, because it was a luxury for him to be there. He felt guilty because he knew he should be helping out at home.

I remember I received all of this with a certain amount of compassion, but also a touch of distracted indifference. Sam had an abrupt way of speaking, and he looked you right in the eye when he talked. I could tell from his tone that he wasn't asking for pity. In fact, I almost felt as though he were challenging me to make the class worthwhile for him. After all, he was making a great sacrifice to be there, and if I didn't deliver the goods, then how could it be worth his effort? I told him I thought it was good that he expected to succeed in school, that it would pay off in the long run, for himself and his family. But I was very much caught up in my own concerns at the moment, the emerging dynamic of the class as a whole, and so we moved on.

These recollections are fleeting, and perhaps enhanced by the knowledge of what came after. But it's safe to say that, while each of my students spoke in class, making some sort of impression upon me that first day, I hadn't yet succeeded in differentiating one from the other. They were a melange of disconnected faces and stories. It wasn't until I read their first essays that it all started to come home a little more.

I remember holding that first batch of essays in my hands, feeling somewhat excited to have all this fresh, clean writing before me, like a tract of forest covered in virgin snow where I would lay down the first prints. I had my brand-new Uniball fine-point marker at the ready, prepared to make encouraging comments, wise asides, helpful suggestions at shaping their raw narratives. But within the hour a feeling of panic had set in. The first few essays I read were all terrible. They lacked imagination, they lacked grammatical construction, but worse yet, they lacked even a sense of idiosyncratic self, the sort of free-wheeling expression of youthful identity that had characterized my own early writings.

It wasn't until about the beginning of the third week of classes that I got around to correcting Sam's essay. His was the second to the last in the pile. I had no reason to expect anything better of it. Sam had continued to make his presence known in class, but not in any way that I found terribly encouraging. At one point I suggested to my students that they might want copies of the "401 Freshman Composition Handbook," which our English department had worked so diligently to compile for them. I hadn't required that anyone read it, but I did want to make it available to my class. So I told them a little of what they might find in it, and held up a copy for anyone who wanted it.

"I'll take one," Sam called out.

I was surprised. Nobody else had shown any interest. He came up, and I handed him the book. After class he was standing by my desk again, handing the book back to me with a grin on his face. "Thanks, Andy," he said. "It was just the right size to keep my desk from rocking back and forth."

I took the book. I was stung. Not so much because he had placed the 401 Handbook, which I didn't really give a damn about anyway, under the leg of his desk to stabilize his chair, but because he had the audacity to actually come up and hand it back to me when he was through. I wanted to say just what I felt at that moment and call him a wiseass. Instead, I smiled back at him and said, "Glad you could put it to good use."

At some point during those fuzzy first two weeks, I made the suggestion that our class would be something like whitewater rafting. I had just gone on such an expedition myself and it seemed to me a great way not only to subtly reveal what a cool, outdoors, sporting sort of guy I was, but to demonstrate how we use metaphor when depicting personal experience. Our class, I told them, would be like going downriver with me as their guide. The five essays they were required to write would be akin to the five sets of class IV rapids I had encountered in my expedition. While the first set of rapids would be frightening, I predicted that with each new rapid we would learn to work more and more as a team, so that, by the final set of rapids we would be in lockstep, negotiating even the trickiest turns with ease.

As I wrapped up this helpful instruction I noticed Sam raising his hand. "Andy, that's a simile, not a metaphor," he informed me. And of course, he was right. I thanked him for his correction and went on with my shattered lesson.

Sam was not afraid to speak his mind. But, at least at that early stage of the class, he rarely said anything productive or relative to the overall discussion. He seemed to enjoy challenging my authority, testing my limits, finding what he could get away with. He didn't know how close he had come to rattling me. And it didn't initially dawn on me that, as a student, Sam had quite a lot to offer.

I was surprised when I got around to reading his first essay. I had become discouraged by my readings thus far, and now, only in the third week, I literally had to rethink my whole approach to how I was going to teach this class. But I remember feeling how Sam's essay had bailed me out. When I finally read it, I jumped up from my chair and did a small victory dance around the kitchen table where I'd been working. I had one student who could actually write, and it was that same annoying kid who kept needling me in class.

His essay was about his father's first major operation. It wasn't great by any means, but it centered itself within a narrative moment, made use of dialogue, and demonstrated a knack for zeroing in on the appropriate details. The essay covered some of the feelings he had talked about on that first day of class. The narrative functioned as an interior monologue while Sam sat in the hospital waiting room, flipping through magazines and fearing the worst. He recalled how his father, upon being wheeled into the OR, called out, "Don't worry, Sam, I'll be pissing like a champ again in no time." This one defiant declaration had helped to pull Sam through. He admired the way his father had used humor to deflect the dire mood, and, how, in his time of trial, he had thought more about Sam's needs than his own.

What I liked most about the essay is that he didn't try to wrap it up neatly at the end. Maybe he couldn't. Everything was so undecided for him. But so many of my students had attempted to draw trite morals from their essays; things like, "I learned to be a better person," or "I realized from my experience that you must live every minute of your life to the fullest." Sam left his essay hanging in the shadow of uncertainty. Yes, he had gained a certain determination to work harder to help his family and shoulder the responsibility for his life. But his narrative remained suspended in doubt, as though he didn't quite know if he was up to the task.

In our first conference I was careful not to pry too deeply into Sam's personal life. We talked about the essay and I told him how much I had liked it. I asked him to dig even deeper into the moment when his father was brought in for surgery, to concentrate only on that day, that hour, the sounds and smells and faces that he encountered while he was in the hospital. Perhaps the most difficult thing I asked of him was not to explain in writing how his father's comment had made him feel. I asked him to leave it out, to let the moment convey the message for us.

I remember how he kept nodding his head, leaning forward in his chair, eyes squinted, as though this information were incredibly dense, hard to take in, and he was straining to comprehend it. "Okay, Andy," was all he said. "I'll give it a try."

Did I believe him at that point? It's hard to say. I had asked similar things of all my students. Many of them nodded their heads in silence, smiling from a deep remove of good intentions mixed with utter incomprehension. I would have to demonstrate to them, over a period of months, that so much of life, so much of our understanding of one another, our love, our hopes, our dreams, our deepest doubts, are conveyed in the silences. That words are, nine times out of ten, ineffectual, but we can order the silences so that they speak as well, and in these spaces our great life stories get told.

Why does a writing teacher preach the aesthetic value of silence, the inadequacy of words, you ask? Because it is only by recognizing this inadequacy that we begin to realize the importance of speaking clearly, of articulating experience in such a way as to overcome the barriers between what is said and what is understood. Sam seemed to comprehend some notion of this. When he had written about his father calling out, "Don't worry, Sam, I'll be pissing like a champ in no time," he knew this utterance suggested more than its surface value would ever allow. He knew it somehow conveyed everything that a father might want to say to a son at such an urgent moment. I think Sam recognized the absurd inadequacy of the words themselves, but also the desperation and hope they were meant to impart as his father was wheeled away from him.

My class was probably good for Sam. It was hard to tell, though. That look on his face, one of dense, even perplexed, concentration, seemed to stay with him for a good part of the semester. He was listening. What's more, he was listening as though I might actually offer him something after all. I had assigned certain readings, like Raymond Carver's "My Father's Life," and a segment from Cormac McCarthy's *All the Pretty Horses,* that dealt with the death of a father, and the way in which the son managed in the wake of this death. Part of my pedagogy was to establish the sense for each of my students that they were witnesses. In the early part of the class, on the first set of rapids, they were merely witnessing their own lives. But as we went on, I hoped to show how we were witness to events as well: tragedies, victories, the lives of friends and lovers. My feeling is that, at some point in every person's life, we will be called upon to witness something. And when that time comes we must be prepared, it is our responsibility to be prepared, and we must have the tools to tell that story. Perhaps it would be, as in the case of Virginia Woolf, the bombing of London. Or it might be, as in the case of Martin Luther King, the racial injustice of Birmingham in the early 1960s. I spoke about Kurt Vonnegut, who witnessed the fire bombing of Dresden, and held it inside for twenty years. For twenty years he knew it was the one story he needed to tell, had a responsibility to tell, but was unable to write of it. He hadn't yet developed the tools, the rhetoric, the uniqueness of perspective that would make such a rendering meaningful. Twenty years to finally write that small but compelling book, *Slaughterhouse Five.*

One day after class, Sam approached me in passing. "I took out that book from the library, by the way," he told me.

"What book?"

"*Slaughterhouse Five.*"

Sam ended up doing his research paper on Vonnegut's life.

I began to feel a sort of connection with Sam, like I was reaching him somehow, beyond the boyish wisecracks and the look of perplexity he often wore in class. His essays grew tighter, began to read like real fledgling novels, and I listened carefully to his words as he slowly developed a fictive voice. In many ways, he reminded me of myself when I was his age, with his subtle disdain for institutional authority, his muted hints of wayward experiences, and the simple fact that he could write.

When Sam wrote about his job, he didn't take you through the mechanical details of the day. He wrote about the people, captured their voices, was attracted to the social misfits he encountered, or the people on the lower rung of the economic ladder, and he listened to their language, tried to understand their codes. In one essay he writes about a guy he worked landscaping with over the summer:

> Jeff gets pissed when he talks about his college days. Not outwardly pissed, but I can tell he's angry. His father was a professor at Elmira College, got him into the business school there. "I did way too many drugs," he says regrettably, "dropped out after a year and a half. Don't get into that shit. It'll mess your life up pretty good, just look at me." I recall stories he's told me about peyote buttons and bad trips, always ending in, "It doesn't make you any smarter."

Sam began to consistently turn in writing like this. I would ask him about his intentions, if he hoped to continue on in English, or if he hoped to keep writing. "I don't know," he would say. "I never gave it any thought."

It was hard for me to get close to Sam. On some level, I wanted to befriend him. I wanted him to take me into his confidence. I wanted to be able to sit down someday and have a casual beer with him and talk about books. I wanted him to say of me what he would go on to say of Jeff in his essay.

Jeff's one of the few people I talk to about my father. As the summer progresses, so does the cancer and the updates become more frequent. Many are uncomfortable when hearing about my misfortunes, but Jeff offers a sort of nonchalant reaction to it which sets me at ease. Sometimes I bitch about not being able to do very much on the weekends because of obligations around the house. Jeff offers no sympathy here though. He says, "You do what you have to to get by."

But I found it hard to break through that student/teacher barrier. It is hard enough to really get to know people under even the best circumstances, and these weren't. Still, as the semester began winding down, I hoped to at least talk to him one last time, tell him that I would be around the next semester if he ever needed someone to chat with, or if the whole process of juggling school and the situation at home ever got too rough.

Maybe I would have said these things to him. Perhaps more than anything else, I wanted some kind of validation from Sam. Had he learned anything? Was this semester-long arc I had constructed to convey the importance of the written language, after all, worth a flying fig? Or was it all pointless? Was writing just another useless exercise in a meaningless world, meant to distract us from the terrifying fact of our own fleeting and insignificant lives?

Silences.

When it came time to hand out the class evaluations, Sam was missing. He hadn't shown up at all for the second to last week of classes. I was disappointed. I wanted, at the very least, to be able to read, at some point, what he had gotten from my class. But he was gone. There was only one class left and he had vanished without a trace, hadn't handed in a final portfolio, hadn't emailed or called. But I found a message in my mailbox that afternoon.

The note just said that I should call him. It was Monday and I called as soon as I got home that evening, fearing the worst. His mother answered the phone. "Sam's father died on Thursday," she told me. "He was with him all last week. He wouldn't leave his side."

"I'm so sorry," I offered.

"Are you his writing teacher?"

"Yeah."

"Sam was so grateful for your class. It really helped him work through this whole thing. He's going to speak at the service tomorrow."

"You have a great son," I told her. "I'm sure he'll have good words to say."

We talked for twenty minutes. She talked; I listened. She talked about Sam and his relationship with his father, how close they had been in those final days. It was one of those surreal moments. I didn't know this woman. I didn't know her husband. But she clearly needed to talk to someone about all these things, and I had called.

So, in the end, maybe I received that validation I'd been looking for. But it came, as successes often do, in such a roundabout, back-stabbing, bittersweet way. And so, by writing this, I become the witness. A witness to Sam and his father, and Sam's development as a writer. I know I couldn't have written as well at his age.

After talking to Sam's mother, I went back to those index cards I had asked my students to fill out on that long-ago first day of classes. I had never looked at them again after reading through them the first time. On each card I had written a little note to help me remember each student. I had forgotten that I'd even done this. On Sam's card I had written, "Father's cancer has helped him mature."

The inadequacy of words.

12

"Gap or Rap"

Class Presence in My First-Year Writing Class

Emily M. Hinnov

Ella had set herself apart from the rest of the class since she shared her very first freewrite during our second class meeting. With no specific writing prompt, Ella wrote a scathing rant about feeling like an outsider in high school. She also elaborated on her anxieties about already feeling the same way at UNH. Although she expressed a lot of the inevitable angst many freshmen feel at the outset of college, it seemed to me that she was quite consciously placing herself in opposition to the "average" first-year student. By average I mean a middle-class white student from a seemingly well-adjusted family in New Hampshire. Apparently, she was constantly called a "freak" at Portsmouth High School because of her numerous piercings and tattoos. To add to that, she shopped at Goodwill and lived in low-income housing while her classmates shopped at the Gap and enjoyed living with well-established families in affluent neighborhoods. She derisively referred to her fellow classmates as either "Gap or rap," her own designations for the typical high school groups she would rather not associate herself with. I distinctly remember the disquieting hush that came over the room as she read from her crumpled sheet of notebook paper with an in-your-face, matter-of-fact tone. She maintained a kind of surface serenity and superiority that I recognized as a guise she must have cultivated to ward off those who had disparaged her so often in the past. Since the moment she shared that freewrite, she continually set herself up as the underdog in our class. I was immediately made uncomfortable by her raw display of emotion, and wondered whether this would be a continual disruption in the smooth-sailing, nonconfrontational classroom dynamic I had hoped my first semester teaching as a Ph.D. candidate would entail.

Soon after that day, Ella and I began our numerous conversations about her feelings of being misunderstood and ostracized by many of her peers, even here at UNH. I listened intently to her spoken confessions and I also gave her a lot of written feedback on her journals. She decided to move out of the dorm and back home, although there is a history of physical abuse there. She changed her major. She worried incessantly about whether she would even continue at UNH. To me, Ella was clearly a bright young woman who was grappling with a plethora of personal issues, and she continually sought to express those struggles, as well as her own views on societal issues, in her writing. Her writing was often quite powerful in its emotional intensity, but we worked on mechanics and clarity of expression for most of the semester. She often shared her rather impassioned points of view on the readings I assigned in our class. I could always count on Ella, whether to my discomfort or pleasure, to start a conversation when my joking attempts to cajole discussion utterly failed.

At about midsemester, we met in my office to discuss her second draft of the research paper. I had asked her if she wanted to workshop it during our next class. She arrived at my door with her customary, somewhat timid, "Hi, Em." She gave a sheepish smile as I offered her the hardback chair. After we'd discussed her questions about revision for a few minutes, she shifted over to the topic of the last assignment, which was a book review. Ella went on about how much she hated this assignment, how she never had to do this kind of critical writing in high school, and how angry she was in the process of writing it. I tried to express my sympathy and to remind her that writing it was an important experience, since she will be asked to do more of this sort of writing in college (this is, of course, my stock answer whenever students resist the idea of analytical writing—which happens *a lot*—and at that moment, it seemed weak even to me). But this protest was nothing new with Ella, since she always came into my office to complain about the writing assignments I gave, which was fine, because I'd much rather have her go off on me than display those possible inadequacies in my planning and pedagogy in front of the entire class.

She reluctantly agreed, but then launched into a complaint about how she overheard a classmate saying that he hadn't actually read the assigned memoir that they had been reading since the beginning of the semester, but had received a higher grade on the paper—even an A. First my gut wrenched, because as always, I immediately assume my own guilt and stupidity when a student challenges the way I make up assignments or grade them. Then I asked Ella how it was possible not to read the book when all the students were required to write weekly journal responses that I collected and then commented on. She responded that since most of the books are bought as used anyway, students could just read the highlighted sections and comment on those. I (probably foolishly) admitted that it upset me as well that some students might not read the whole book, but also admitted that there wasn't much I could really do about that. I was absolutely fuming inside, and that fact was most likely visible in my trembling hands and my reddening cheeks, so I recrossed my legs, plucked a piece of stray hair off my shoulder, and tried to appear calm. All I could think about was the fact that we all read texts differently, with different levels of attention, and that I, as an "English person" for most of my life, know that many of us learn how to bullshit pretty well without reading the entire text. The fact remained that those students who received an A on the book review assignment (and those two were the most outstanding writers in the class) just wrote better papers, period. It didn't ultimately matter that someone else had read the text with more care or labored more closely with it.

Was Ella just looking for sympathy here? I told her that I understood how frustrating it could be to feel that you worked harder on an assignment than someone who seemingly breezed through it and got a better grade. I admitted that I had often felt the same way. She looked somewhat relieved, yet still aggravated, and somehow expectant. She looked like she was hoping that I might change her grade because she had let me in on this vital, top secret information. But we needed to get back to the research paper at hand. As I prodded her more about her plans for revision on that paper, my interior paranoia rambled on. *Oh God, does she expect me to change her grade? Is she trying to tell me in some subtle way that I am an idiot not to see that students had not read the book? Is this a challenge to my already somewhat tenuous (and often faked) authority? Does she think I would ask her the name of the student and take some sort of substantial action? If so, what does she expect me to do? And worst of all, will she no longer think I'm a cool teacher who happens to listen to Radiohead, too?*

OK, even if the story I was getting was not filtered through her (possibly) skewed perspective, this was clearly not a case of plagiarism. I decided, after obsessing with my office-mate and my equally self-critical grad student friend, that I didn't need to feel like I should take some sort of action, and that Ella was really just sour grapes about the assignment. I assured myself that I needed to rely on my own instinct about those other papers, knowing that I honestly couldn't even imagine that those two students who received A's could have neglected to read the book. I was grading the quality of their writing anyway, wasn't I? Even if they had not read the book, so what? They were better able to spin a strong response and analysis from whatever they read than Ella was. But of course I still felt guilty about Ella's added burden of feeling an outsider who could never quite click with the rest of the students.

And to make things even more harrowing for my already weak self-confidence here, I couldn't help but think that Ella's social class had finally crept into her perhaps overly suspicious feelings of being the inadequate under-dog, the struggling underclass in our English 401 class. Even once I understood how Ella's lower-working-class family affected her behavior with other students and with me, the one teacher she had seen it fit to approach with her personal problems, I was still uncomfortable and reticent about how to handle it. But I don't believe that I was misperceiving Ella's performance here. She received a B— on that book review paper, mainly because she continued to struggle with issues of precision and grammar that marred the readability of her writing, and those problems were still evident in that final draft, even after we had worked through many of them in conference earlier. I am quite conscious of my role as an instructor in reinforcing the social order in the classroom, and strive not to do so in a way that marginalizes anyone, mostly because I can relate more closely to a student with Ella's background than I can to some more privileged kid who went to Phillips Exeter Academy. I was often that cynical girl in high school (and some of early college, when I was a "goth chick" who dyed my hair black and wore used Doc Marten boots), especially when I saw typically moneyed Danvers High School students driving their shiny new cars, wearing their hip new Gap outfits, and getting college paid for by their parents. We barely had heat in a house I was embarrassed for even close friends to enter, I too had to work from the time I was fourteen (my first social security–earning job was at the local Dunkin' Donuts, where I was forced to wear the circa 1977 polyester jumpsuit uniform—complete with a striking array of orange, brown, and pink donut trees), and I had to take out college loans that I'll be paying off at the good old Sallie Mae Corporation until I'm fifty-five. That camaraderie I thought I shared with Ella, the one that made me feel like she regarded me as her "cool" college instructor, was one of the reasons I tried to be sensitive to her issues and had often lent a willing ear to her excessive venting. I wanted to introduce her draft in a class workshop to show her that she wasn't quite the low young woman on the totem pole, at least when it came to her writing, as she might have thought she was. I wanted her to realize that those deep-seated feelings of inadequacy did not have to hamper her ability to express them, and any others, through her writing. I wanted her to experience the empowerment of her words while also being aware of the fact that they stem from that class-consciousness. What I really should have done was to encourage her to tackle the class issue in her research essay. I felt too anxious about it at the time. Class is something that is difficult for everyone to talk about. Even now, when my bitterness erupts at friends who have trust funds and I am embarrassed by alternately voicing and concealing my "white trash" upbringing, I don't know how to handle this issue in a college classroom. In this post-PC age, we can talk about race, gender, and sexuality, but we still can't seem to discuss class. It just makes people extremely uncomfortable.

But on the other hand, how far should I have gone in helping her feel validated? I couldn't help but think that in that conference, she was trying to manipulate the sympathy I'd expressed for her situation in the past. It felt like a trap to me, and I couldn't shake the uneasiness that ensued from that meeting. I couldn't in any good conscience allow her any special exceptions just because she felt persecuted, even if I felt like I understood where her class position placed her in the unspoken hierarchy. Could I have done any more than show compassion, encourage her strengths, and gently remind her of her weaknesses as a writer? Would it have been enough to assure her that she was right, that it's not true that everyone who works hard and pulls himself up by his bootstraps will have any more success than the person who just knows better how to play the game? This is America after all, but that American Dream no longer exists, no matter how much we want to believe otherwise.

From my perspective, she blended in more closely with the rest of the students in my class than her exaggerated sense of her difference made it seem. She was often a leader in the class discussions we had about the readings. Her classmates expressed admiration for her willingness to voice strong points of view in class and in her writing. But that feeling of unease cannot quite be resolved for me. I'm sure that if I hadn't been reminded of my own past while this situation was unfolding, I would have been more likely to chalk Ella's behavior up to "just dealing with another difficult student" without perhaps looking beneath the surface for the origins of that dilemma. Here at least I could see that her sense of disenfranchisement was strongly tied to her experience of growing up as a lower-class young woman, maybe even poverty-stricken, in a fairly prosperous community. Yet this realization doesn't change the fact that I still don't know how to better handle a situation like this one.

13

A Language in Letters

Learning to Communicate Honestly Through Grades

Kelly Myers

Growing up I noticed that in the dad world when there are no more words, when there is no more logic, there is "because I said so." I understand that I was not the only child to fall victim to this unjust term, but I didn't understand that as a kid. All I wanted from my dad was an explanation—a concrete reason why he had closed the door on my hopes with this final, irreversible, *completely vague* judgment. The answer to my endless pleas for justice was always the same: "Because I said so." I felt cheated, wronged, dominated. I felt like my thoughts and opinions didn't matter. Although my dad has given more justified explanations than "said so's" in his career as my father, I decided at a young age that I would do my part to protect the world from this dad treatment... And then I became a teacher. Though I didn't have fatherly confidence backing up my "because I said so," I was, for the most part, espousing that same torturous sentiment during my first semester of teaching. This is a C paper... because it is, because I, uh, said so.

I walked into my teaching career at twenty-three years old, not long after walking across the stage with my college diploma. Dorm rooms, meal plans, co-ed bathrooms, and small wooden desks did not feel that far away. Obsessing over the threat of a GPA-devastating B+ was not at all far away. But then suddenly there I was, holding GPA devastators in the palm of my hand. There I was, sitting at the big desk with a grade book and no idea how to use it. As both a graduate student and a teacher, I knew how to get good grades, but not how to give them. I knew how to discover and produce exactly what my teachers wanted, but had no idea what I wanted from students. I knew how to analyze and discuss writing, but I did not know how to explain writing or lead an effective discussion. I was the grader and the graded, the creator of syllabi and the one for whom syllabi are created. I didn't know which persona to choose. When I found myself analyzing the organization and presentation (rather than the course requirements) of a graduate-level syllabus, I felt the reality of an identity crisis sinking in. I was juggling two lives, feeling as if the graded had no business dealing out grades.

In dealing with my grading dilemma, I became my father. I "because I said so-ed" twenty-four teenagers on a regular basis, giving grades without enough explanation to back up my decisions. A party to the idea that students cannot write freely once branded with a letter grade, I did not give any grades in the beginning. Around midsemester, when my students could no longer tolerate the darkness and insecurity in which they were living, I conceded a hypothetical grading system, but refused to be too harsh in my commentary. As I "graded," I worked feverishly to pick out anything positive I could find to comment on, but I always made sure that the final grade complied with university standards. According to the university's policy, a C is an average grade; according to most college freshmen, a C is heartbreaking. Thus, my commentary ended up looking something like this:

> Jill,
>
> Really nice work! I like the way that you have used voice and detail in places. There is some beautiful writing in this piece. Interesting topic. Good ideas.
>
> "If" I were to grade this: B—

I doubt that Jill picked up on the underlying message that she used good voice and detail only *in places* and that *some* beautiful writing does not mean that the entire piece is well written. But I am sure that she noticed the glaring B—. I was (unknowingly) slamming the door on hopes, denying explanation, making students feel as if their thoughts and opinions didn't matter—but truth be told, I was just scared.

In English 401 at the University of New Hampshire, students are never just numbers or faces in a crowd. Teachers *know* their students. Through their work my students invite me into their homes, introduce me to their parents and pets, let me run around in their backyards, show me their broken hearts, invite me to prom. I know their style, habits, and sense of humor. The vague and seemingly unfair grading of my first semester came from stepping too lightly around human emotion. I centered my class on the personal narrative and made the mistake of taking it too personally. In conference I listened to my students very carefully—to the point where I could hear their voices as I graded their work. Knowing the battles that I have fought with my own confidence as a writer, I did not want to discourage my students in any way. I ended up giving all A's and a handful of B+'s my first semester, not realizing that rather than encouraging students to write I was actually leading them on, setting them up for future disappointment.

When I filled out my final grade sheet that first semester, I convinced myself that my students had worked really hard and deserved such high-grade rewards. Looking back, I know that most of my students did work hard, but hard work does not always produce extraordinary writing. It all comes back to my singing career. For the past two decades I have been a closet rock star. I have spent long hours in shower, car, and locked bedroom venues, fine-tuning my singing voice. To this day, my only public performances have been car radio duets—and for good reason. My singing voice is shockingly bad. I have worked *really hard* at it, but I am not a good singer. If I am ever going to have a decent singing voice, I need some help. I need a teacher who will listen to my voice and help me hit the right notes—a teacher who will appreciate my work ethic, but honestly tell me how I sound.

I want to be liked, as most of us do, and this need for popularity makes it difficult to grade honestly. I will never forget the professor who gave me a B in college. I enjoyed both him and his class all semester, but part of me has loathed him ever since the final grades were issued, four years ago. Grades are *earned,* but very few students can or will take responsibility. I earned that B, but I automatically placed blame on the "tyrannical teacher" and his "unfair grading system." It is never fun to feel like the tyrannical teacher. When I see a former student who earned a low grade in my class, I still want to run and hide. Sometimes it is difficult for students and teachers alike to remember that grades are a form of communication, not weaponry. Sometimes shields, sometimes knives, grades are often viewed as devices to protect or puncture student egos. It may be nearly impossible to grade a student's work without hearing the voices of their attributes and flaws, but the important part is to proceed with honest commentary, seeking an extra set of English teacher eyes if necessary.

To grade honestly, we have to push our egos and our students' egos aside. While giving D's and F's may feel like more of a risk, the real danger lies on the other end of the grading scale. Students believe A's. They tend to fight or ignore D's and F's but believe A's without question. An A student is someone who has mastered the material and developed exemplary skills. An A can allow a student to feel comfortable, even complacent, with the level of knowledge attained. If we inflate grades, we may create students who falsely believe that the rules of revision and constructive criticism do not apply to them. It is important to remember that these students will go on to have other teachers in their college career and will, at some point, have to be taught.

There is a lurking problem with grade inflation, a problem that wears the face of each and every teacher on campus—teachers who could potentially have an inflated grade/inflated ego writer in class. Since writing stretches all the way across campus, dipping its fingers into every subject, the truth will eventually come out. Timid graders turn honest graders into villains. When my college professor gave me a B, I figured there could only be one reason: he hated me. Somewhere along the line I had gotten myself onto his bad side and ultimately paid the price. I considered myself the victim of an angry man's rage. Looking back I can see that I did B-level work in his class and received an accurate evaluation—nothing personal. In reality, I was the victim of an overly generous freshman English teacher who gave me a false sense of security, dazzling me with straight A's, blinding me from all that I had left to learn. Grading honestly may jeopardize student/teacher trust during the semester, but grade inflation puts a grander scale of student/teacher trust at risk.

I don't enjoy it when students lie to me. I can hear it in their voices and read it in their body language: "My printer just suddenly ran out of ink without warning, so I could only print out a page and a half...." Ah, of course. Although their missed alarm clock, crashed computer, "my dorm room ate my essay" excuses are tough to take, aren't we doing the same thing when we inflate their grades? Aren't we dancing around the truth, trying to survive the semester with our hands clean of student disappointment? As I said earlier, *grades are a form of communication*. Giving average work an above-average grade is a miscommunication and if we do it knowingly, it's a lie. A student who receives an inflated grade may feel like a good writer and have the confidence to keep writing, but if that student did not really learn the tools of good writing, he or she will eventually be caught in the lie.

As writing teachers, we are helping students pack for the collegiate journey ahead, making sure that they are outfitted with the proper English equipment. We lay out a good supply of reading and writing practice, critical and creative thinking skills, research methods and tools, but students ultimately decide what they will carry with them. Grades should reflect both what our students have taken and what they have left behind.

3

Challenging Authority

Facing Resistance in the Classroom

Sometimes we talk about *the* class, or the students who still surprise us with visits to our office, phone calls, or Christmas cards. There are students whose eyes light up when we pass them on campus, who stop to talk about their semesters, who remind us what wonderful teachers we are, remind us that we made a difference. When we talk about those students our heads swell. We wonder why, while walking briskly back to Hamilton Smith Hall, we haven't won some kind of award. Perhaps they should move us into that corner office, give us that personal secretary that, as the best teacher in the university, we so obviously deserve. Ah yes, super teachers that we are, we strut into the classroom, all confidence . . . then we see the face, the eyes that narrow in at us. Our heads deflate; we know that look. He's sitting there, holding our gaze, waiting to see who breaks first. And we are again put back into our place. Oh yeah, we remind ourselves, *him*.

It will come. If you don't get him or her your first semester, you will your second or third. He's sitting in the back corner now, arms crossed, baseball hat tipped below eye level. Or she's sitting in the front with a smirk, sharing a glance with her friend when you say something that you think is hilarious. You notice the smirk, you cough and continue. When did I become such a dork, you wonder.

You'll get her.

You'll get him.

The resistant student.

Just thought we'd warn you.

We're not psychologists; we don't know why they resist us. Could it be that they're jealous of our striking good looks, our remarkable sense of humor, our stunning intelligence? Perhaps, but doubtful. It may be a control thing, a lack of self-esteem that triggers this passive- or aggressive-aggression. We ask our students to be critical readers, critical thinkers, critical writers. We want them to question the world around them, interrogate norms, analyze everything. That's fine . . . until that critical eye gets turned on us. And we panic.

Welcome to teaching.

In reading this section you'll get a good idea of the diversity of resistant students: some are aggressive, some are passive-aggressive, some are flat-out bullies, some just don't show up to class, some bombard us with explanatory emails and an endless list of personal dramas. You'll see, also, the different ways teachers deal with resistant students. These authors invite you to follow the semester to see where they stumbled, where they failed, where they succeeded, and where they still feel as though there's unfinished business.

14

The Gospel According to Luke

Alexei Di Orio

Flipping through the first stack of personal essays that I received after my first week of teaching freshman composition, I was pleasantly surprised by my students' willingness to reveal themselves by describing critical, traumatic, lucid moments of their lives and how they processed them emotionally. One paper, Luke's, stood out from the rest, for three reasons. It described a strangely *impersonal* experience, one that might have even been invented for the purpose of the assignment (Luke relates how as a child, he put his hands on a boiling pot of water, burned himself, and learned to be more careful in the future). It was also more stylistically sophisticated than most of the other papers in the stack. Finally, it was only a page and a half, less than half the length that I had asked for in this first assignment.

While I found Luke's first piece curious, I was more intrigued by the uniqueness of his voice than I was alarmed or annoyed at his deviation from my assignment. This was soon to change, as we had our first sustained period of face-to-face contact in the second week of classes, during our first round of conferences. Several dissonant tones emerged from this first exchange between Luke and me, a dissonance that would haunt us for the remainder of the semester. First, he was completely resistant to the virtues of revision that I had preached during the first week. My agenda for that first round of conferences was to locate some points in the rough draft that might serve as foci for further development. I prodded him to tell me more about the incident he described in his essay, but he insisted that he had completely exhausted his topic: there was nothing left to write. He dismissed each suggestion I offered for development and kept deflecting my questions right back at me. I tried to get him to fill in some of the conceptual blanks of his paper, think more critically about his experience, explore some new directions in his writing, but he would dodge and weave from my prompts, repeatedly asking me which particular sentence or word needed fixing or cutting. Revision for Luke seemed to be a matter of purging his draft of stylistic or grammatical impurities, approaching the Platonic ideal of a good personal experience essay, the qualities of which I was obstinately, perversely withholding from him—that is, he was expressing precisely the attitude toward writing that I had been urging my students to reject in that first week of classes.

A second issue that cropped up in this exchange was Luke's refusal to reveal anything personal about himself in his writing. The frustrating dialogue on revision led me to suspect that a more interesting topic might be in order, one that he felt more personally connected to. I felt entitled to ask for a change of topic and a new essay from Luke, since he had delivered only a fraction of the five pages that the assignment called for. Contrary to the mantra that I had repeated ceaselessly in class ("there's no such thing as a bad topic"), I wondered if we were hitting a brick wall because Luke's topic was so oddly impersonal, if we could make some progress by pursuing a more emotionally or intellectually resonant topic.

Instead of spontaneously generating a list of ideas for new topics, incidents of interest in Luke's life that he might explore, we just hit the wall again, but with more violence this time. Just as he had insisted that he had nothing left to say about his chosen topic, he drew a blank on potentially rich incidents in his life that he might develop into a substantial essay. Clearly, the issue here was not a lack of interesting or meaningful experiences to write about, but rather a reluctance to share them with *me* or other readers. The awkwardness of the conference, with long lulls between questions that Luke refused to answer directly, was getting to me by this point. I grew impatient with his stubbornness, his habit of looking at his shoes while we talked, his determination to leave my office without surrendering an inch of ground to me. Eventually, I told him that the draft that I had read just wasn't all that interesting, because it lacked any connection to the author's life. I couched that message in terms of the issue of audience: there was nothing to charge a reader's interest in Luke's draft, since he described such a common, impersonal experience and squeezed so little significance out of it.

Luke immediately struck a defensive posture when I pointed to this inadequacy in his essay, retorting, "So am I supposed to *entertain you* in my paper?" I took this question to challenge both the seriousness of the assignment (the essay is meant to *entertain*; we weren't working to produce effective personal essays, we were just playing, swapping fun stories) and my seriousness as a teacher (the essay is meant to entertain *me*; my standards for good writing were a totally arbitrary matter of whether or not a piece engaged my fickle attention span). Luke's question, which I took as naked insolence, threw me off completely. Like Luke, I had nothing left to say, no defense prepared to justify my suggestions for revision. So I told him rather sternly that everyone else in the class managed to produce a *five*-page essay on a *personal* event of significance, and he needed to go back to the drawing board if he wanted to satisfy the assignment. On the whole, I thought my other twenty-three conferences went swimmingly. I was pleased with my newfound ability to strike a reasonably "teacherly" pose in each conference; my students seemed to find my revision suggestions helpful, insightful, and most importantly, for me, *authoritative*. Luke's conference is the only one that I remember clearly months later, though, because he directly, though no doubt unintentionally, challenged this authority that I was desperately trying to muster in my class. His resistance to the process of revision struck at my rather deep insecurities concerning my qualifications to teach the class. I couldn't offer him a satisfyingly concrete, empirical answer to his recurrent question, "What's *wrong* with my paper?" Maybe there was no substance to the process that I was urging my students to appreciate, only my own arbitrary sense of what works and what doesn't work in a piece of writing. I took myself to task for handling Luke so brusquely toward the end of that conference. He was obviously a serious, reserved kid who didn't want me, or anyone else, sticking my nose into his business, so why did I insist that he try harder to reveal himself in his writing? Freshman composition isn't a therapy session, after all, it's a writing class. Demanding that a student offer a confession to the teacher seemed rather sadistic and indefensible. The point of the assignment wasn't to wrench such private revelations out of my students, of course, and it drove me crazy to think that Luke saw my intentions as essentially voyeuristic.

I was able to make a respectable recovery with Luke the next day, when I bumped into him in the library and talked briefly about the issues that emerged from our conference. I offered him a few more options for a change of topic: tell me a funny story, tell me about an interesting character you've run across, or an event that has a general interest, a trip that you took, a scene that you witnessed. I stressed that the essay needn't be personal in the self-revealing or -diagnosing sense, but only as an occasion to draw on his life's experience in his writing. This correction went over well with Luke and he seemed to feel less daunted by the prospect of coming up with five pages of new material. My earlier diagnosis was confirmed: the resistance that I had encountered the day before was primarily a result of Luke's unwillingness to speak of his emotional life publicly. Luke also frankly expressed his skepticism concerning the ultimate value of this particular class. He was pre-law and didn't understand how it might relate to his career goals, to the "real world." Here I retreated from my earlier insistence that the personal essay was a crucial mode of self-expression and tried to sell him on other writing skills that we would work on later in the semester that would respond directly to those goals (writing a research paper, analyzing the persuasive arguments of others in our readings, constructing our own, and so on).

I felt like I had made some progress with Luke with this recovery in the library, and it seemed that our struggle had already lost its edge. In particular, Luke seemed to respond well to the extra attention I had given him. I think that Luke found my directives less arbitrary and impossible to satisfy after I had promised to make myself available to work through those moments of confusion or inertia in the writing process. Truth be told, I felt like Teacher of the Year after that exchange: I had succeeded in reaching out to a "difficult" student. But the conflict would erupt again soon afterward, when I read the cover letter that Luke attached to his second draft, explaining changes that he made between the two drafts. He writes,

> The main reason I did the paper over was at the request of my teacher. There
> was also a problem with the length of the paper, which was significantly less
> than the required amount. Due to the fact that the experience was a short one
> it seemed logical just to do the assignment over. However looking back I think
> I liked the first one better because I think I explained much more of who I am
> in much less space. The second one was larger in quantity but I don't think
> it explained myself as much as the previous. The second however is more
> entertaining perhaps to the reader than the first, which perhaps is an important
> factor in a piece of writing.

Here Luke politely suggests that I had steamrolled him into churning out a
piece that he didn't like, abandoning a piece that he did like, one that "explained
much more of who [he is] in much less space." The term "entertaining" is a
direct echo from our previous conference, and it hit a nerve, since he clearly
still judged the interest factor in writing to be a dubious virtue (note the two
uses of "perhaps" in the concluding sentence). I have to disagree with Luke's
self-assessment, though. His second draft was much stronger than his first one,
even if it was written under duress. He chose to pursue my suggestion and
write a humorous (but impersonal, once again) story about a road trip he took
with his friends. In our second round of conferences, we fell right back into the
earlier rhythm. I prodded him to add more detail to his piece, while he stoically
resisted my suggestions. I asked him to describe more fully the friends he had
mentioned only by name in his piece. We went through an infuriating and futile
interrogation session as Luke gave me strangely impersonal details about his
friends (hair color, height, and such) that couldn't possibly interest a reader. It
was here that I decided that Luke just didn't get it; I was wasting my time with
him, and we were facing a semester that would be unbearable for both of us.

    The next skirmish between Luke and me would be our bloodiest one, from
my perspective, at least. The second major writing assignment was a three-
to four-page piece on a significant learning experience, and I was astonished
to find Luke telling me about *himself* in his essay, in a mode that illuminated
some of the teacher/student conflicts that we were having. He describes how
he had an epiphany after reading *The Catcher in the Rye* in seventh grade,
which taught him to be both idealistic and intolerant of "phoniness" in the
world. He describes his high school experiences in extremely bleak terms. He
"read religiously," working through heady books of philosophy and literature,
meanwhile earning wretched grades in school because his teachers (English
teachers, significantly) wanted him only to jump through mindless hoops and
didn't care what he thought:

> I wrote a 20-page thesis/research paper that examined what a genius is, their
> role in society, and how they are treated today. I showed her [the English
> teacher] how her classroom didn't foster creativity or creative thought. For

subject matter I got an A. However, because my bibliography wasn't typed correctly I got a C for an overall grade. She said it didn't matter what I said, it was how I presented it and although I made some interesting points they had no purpose in the real world. This grade had me flunk honors English.

This is the point where I broke down. I entered a state of depression and stopped doing all work. What was the use of having all this knowledge if I had no use for it? I didn't care anymore what grades I got because nobody cared about what I thought. It was as if people didn't want to be helped.

He goes on to relate how his parents sent him to a psychiatrist after this breakdown, and forced him to work a degrading job to straighten him out. Eventually he broke with his Salinger-inspired idealism and decided to become a lawyer, to pursue power and money instead of trying to help people break out of their phoniness.

It was a fascinatingly odd piece, and I felt like Luke had equipped me to read the resistance he was giving me in our class. His prose was bitter, egotistical, and sarcastic, but vigorously honest. He seemed righteous about his adoption of "Holden's" worldview and entitled to evangelize the world after seeing the light. In a revised version, he would use the allegory of the cave from Plato's *Republic* to describe how "society" rejected his words of wisdom, choosing to remain in darkness. It was also a rather pathetic piece, revealing how completely miserable he was throughout high school and how he currently sees himself as killing time as an undergraduate until he can become a lawyer: "All I want now is a piece of paper saying I'm a lawyer so I can get a lot of green paper that says I don't have to listen to anybody."

The contradictions embedded in this essay are bafflingly rich. Luke presents himself as the passive victim of others' insensitivity, poignantly indicating moments of deep humiliation in his life, but he also draws attention to his perpetual underachievement. His presentation is rhetorically sophisticated, but he seems blind to the holes in his argument. For example, in the preceding extract, he seems to be deliberately provoking his English teacher by telling her how worthless her class is, and yet he expects us to sympathize with him when he earns a lower grade. He seems very world-weary at age eighteen, brimming with hostility toward "the stupid, ignorant, and unjust," but it's a pretty immature philosophy, obviously. In short, he invites the reader to sympathize with him through his candor, his sense of outrage against injustice, and his background of being victimized, but at the same time, he alienates his reader through his egotism (presuming to enlighten the masses as a high school student) and the flimsiness of his argument (essentially, that his bad experience with the English teacher started a chain reaction of traumatic events that robbed him of his chance to go to a better college like Dartmouth or Berkeley).

I was fascinated with this essay in light of my earlier experiences with Luke, but I wasn't sure what my next move should be. I was turned off by the egotism and shallowness of his "philosophy," his resignation to "jumping through hoops" for the next four years of his undergraduate education, and the note of right-wing elitism that ran through his piece (suggesting that he was meant to attend a better college, slurs against the working-class guys that he was forced to work with during that traumatic stage, invoking Ayn Rand, of all people, as one of those idealist writers who helped formed his worldview). I was also forced to wonder what this piece said about his impressions of *me*: was I being interpellated here as the latest in a series of unimaginative English teachers who didn't care what Luke thought and expected only dull obedience from him? Was he trying to manipulate me, maybe arguing that only a dim-witted teacher would fail to recognize his brilliance and give him a C? Or that only a callous monster of a teacher would contribute to his psychic scarring by failing to give him the A that he should have received in high school?

But on the other hand, his essay was honest and revealing, describing his pain and failures, if in a detached, cynical style. It was well written, with great descriptions of his inner life during his high school years, and a promisingly acid style that was hard to dislike entirely. It also represented a moment of progress after our earlier *tête-à-tête*. Luke seemed genuinely interested in telling his story, going a few pages over the minimal assignment after a series of thin papers that rarely hit the target length. He had disproved his claim that he had "nothing to say."

With this ambivalence toward Luke's paper in mind, I decided to write a very short but encouraging comment on his paper: "I like the *honesty* of this piece and the bitterness that you sustain. . . . I'm happy to see you putting more of *yourself* in your writing." I was soon forced to be a bit tougher on him, though, when he handed in exactly the same five pages as the first draft for a new assignment, another five-page personal experience essay. Essentially, he had nothing to show for at least a week's worth of work. On one draft, I wrote to Luke,

So I've got your first draft of the 2nd essay and your learning experience piece from last week in front of me, and I'm not seeing any changes or effort at revising. You did exactly what I told everyone *not* to do, just pass in a second copy of that earlier essay. It's fine w/ me if you wanted to keep working on that piece, but I told you I wanted 3–4 pages of *new* material . . . so if you want credit for this assignment, I expect that new stuff forthwith.

Putting that issue aside, however, I like the essay and I wanted to hear more about these experiences & your connection to the book [*Catcher in the Rye*]. I was left wondering whether or not your resentment towards, well, everyone, it seems, has mellowed over the years, or do you still see the world acc. to Salinger's view, people who "get it" on the one hand vs. all the "phonies" on the other hand? I guess I'd like to see a bit more depth to what you've got so far, rethinking those high school experiences. You're entitled to your own view of the world, of course, but there's an arrogant streak running through your piece (arrogance isn't necessarily a bad thing in writing, though), which suggests that, basically, everyone you've met is a moron or is out to get you, and I'm wondering if that's *really* what you think *now*: has your worldview evolved over the years? Do you think that that 16-year-old view of the world (when you read the book & adopted it as "your Bible") is good enough, not worth questioning, etc.?

I stand by my appraisal of his piece, where "arrogant" is a polite word for his over-the-top egomania. It seemed right to put some pressure on that misanthropic worldview that he had laid out in his paper, but pressure in the context of revising the essay, defending and expanding on those cynical implications if he meant them, clarifying himself or adding a retrospective turn if he didn't. It also seemed fair to demand a bit more of him in light of the sophistication of his writing and his self-presentation as a misunderstood intellectual and seeker-after-truth.

Luke would throw back the gauntlet in his cover letter to the second draft of the essay, which was supposed to account for the changes he made between drafts:

I didn't change my 2nd draft from my 1st draft. Here are several reasons why. Firstly the suggestions you gave me to change my piece seem invalid. I'm going to respond to these suggestions first.

A. I don't resent everyone. I think the essay clearly shows that the resentment is toward ignorance.

B. The resentment hasn't mellowed. If you reread the sentence you underlined "All I want now is a piece of paper saying I'm a lawyer so I can get a lot of green paper that says I don't have to listen to anybody." It means I don't want to have any part to do with the ignorant, instead of helping them overcome their ignorance.

C. I don't agree that Salinger had a "get it" philosophy and therefore have no intention on elaborating on it. . . .

I'm afraid why you may have frustration leading me through the draft process is because I almost literally do it every paper. Most of my time is just spent trying to see the paper. I'll sit for perhaps an hour visualizing the paper in my head and I won't start writing till I know exactly what I want my paper to say and how I want to say it. . . .

So you can see I do the entire writing process each time I write a paper. . . . It seems that you are punishing me because I don't do the process like you want me to and that's bad judgment on your part. Who are you to say what is the right way to write? Even if you were an eminent writer your opinion would still be invalid because you will never be an expert on my thought process and therefore never have the right to tell me how I should write. Especially considering my writing is good and at the risk of sounding arrogant most people will agree that I write well.

I don't think the same way as everyone else. That's why I'm not at Dartmouth or Berkeley. However, that's the same reason why I'm not still scraping gum off the floor.

A. I'm still not going to change this paper because I'm sure almost anything I change or add will degrade it.

B. I'm not going to degrade my paper until you tell how you want it done in writing conference. This is because I won't degrade it until I'm positive I'll receive a good grade for doing so.

If I was confused about what to do with Luke earlier in the semester, now I was starting to panic. I was also absolutely livid at his multifaceted and open attack against my authority (possibly my intelligence as well). I fumed and stomped around for an hour or so after reading Luke's manifesto, soliciting advice from colleagues as to how (if) I should respond. While in retrospect, I doubt that his intentions were to reveal any lack of respect for me and my class, I was sure at the time that he was directly trying to engage me in a bizarre little power struggle.

What got under my skin here (beyond the jab that I wasn't qualified to give him advice on his writing, since I wasn't an "eminent writer") was the dogmatism of Luke's gesture, his conviction that his writing skills had reached their zenith, his argument that he had already processed all the variables of his essay mentally and the writing process was a waste of his time. Essentially, we were back to square one. He had said what he meant, he had meant what he said, so what's the point of revising or rethinking his piece? I also felt like Luke might be trying to manipulate me again: instead of doing the work that everyone else in the class had managed to accomplish without complaint, he was proposing a (far-fetched) argument that excused him from the assignment.

I had an understandably tense conference with Luke the next day. I found it impossible to focus on the writing and offer suggestions about his piece when addressing those basic issues of authority and respect seemed to be the task of the moment. And since Luke had already decided that I wasn't an "eminent writer," of course, the possibility of my suggestions having any value had already been eliminated. Luke was about two weeks behind in his writing at this point, since he had passed in exactly the same paper three times. He backed off a little in conference, stressing that he wasn't trying to attack me personally—he just couldn't see how his essay could be changed. We sank into our accustomed rhythm, as I prodded Luke unsuccessfully into "unpacking" some of the comments he made in his essay and he responded with determined resistance. It went horribly.

I wasn't sure at this point how much of our struggle was due to my inexperience as a teacher, how much to Luke's attitude problems. I decided to reach out to him once again before giving up completely on the project of getting through to him. I wrote out an exhaustive, line-by-line commentary on the essay that I had received three times already, four pages of questions that were designed to provoke Luke to reconsider underargued or underdeveloped points in his piece. My comments were tough; I demanded that he defend some of the more outlandish comments he made in his paper:

> Your comments on how you decided to become a lawyer seem pretty extreme. Your parents made you work a humiliating job and that somehow taught you that you need to take advantage of people? Your logic here is pretty fuzzy and needs elaboration. Did you ever actually *help* anyone, by the way? You claim that you were so idealistic & ready to share your wisdom, and that philanthropic impulse led to disaster, but what did that impulse amount to, really? Your argument seems to be, "I tried to be idealistic and failed, I was punished for my generous impulses, so therefore I might as well become a lawyer, be successful & rich if I can't change the world": But what did you *do*, beyond read a few books in high school and write about them in a couple of papers? Did you really *try*? In other words, your conclusion seems really weak & tenuous, an *excuse*.

The issue here was not the inadequacy of Luke's worldview (which I found obnoxious, to be sure), but rather his insistence that his first draft was perfect and revision was totally unnecessary. My (absurdly) extended remarks were meant to serve as a demonstration that dozens of different directions for an essay might appear if one would interrogate one's writing completely and probingly, and there's no such thing as a perfect first draft. I was surprised at the success of my maneuver: Luke was impressed by the time I spent in addressing his case and my willingness to give him a few extra days to produce a revised version. It was a rather hollow victory when Luke finally turned in a draft that contained some significant changes, since beyond the issue of teaching him the value of interrogating his writing, there lurked a suspicion that he was merely jumping through hoops again, getting by with the minimal requirement to satisfy the teacher and earn his B+.

This was my last significant clash with Luke. Thereafter, we addressed each other with toleration and civility, but he still was determined to get through the class with the bare minimum of work. In his reader responses, he would routinely take a turn that would bar the possibility of further thought or writing. For example, he ends his discussion of a piece by Margaret Atwood on pornography with the terse statement, "I'm not an expert on porn so I won't argue with her." Finis. Often, I would be startled by a great sentence or two in his writing, only to be disappointed when he abruptly broke off the piece. In his response to an article on how social class is never treated explicitly in American high schools, he offers this wonderful metaphor:

> It's like Western Civilization is an intricate sweater that has been being woven for over a hundred years. There's a loose thread though and out of curiosity people like to see what the sweater is made out of. They pull it and pull it until all there is left is a pile of wool yarn. Great, we know what the sweater is made up of and how it was made but we've lost sight of why it was made.

This sweater which has been painstakingly woven by generations to keep the next generation warmer is now just a useless pile of yarn. Now everybody is cold. I suppose the moral of the story is not to pull loose strands of society unless you know what's going to happen.

While I find the politics of Luke's metaphor a bit repellent, I was pleased to see his curiosity in following that "thread" of thought . . . and displeased when he stopped writing, since the assignment called for twice the amount of material that he produced. Luke's research paper was extremely odd, too. His first topic was "polyethylene," which seemed to be a deliberate challenge against my directive that students try to find a subject that relates to their lives somehow and would engage their curiosity for a full five weeks. When he couldn't find any sources for that topic, he decided to research Buddhism. The final product was a thin mixture of his own free associations about religion, his analysis of Maugham's *The Razor's Edge*, and some light encyclopedia-based research. His paper was totally contemptuous of the assigned length and format; it was mainly a disappointing skim along the surface of Eastern religion (which led me to wonder what Luke's high school paper on "the genius in society" might have looked like).

I would handle a case like Luke's differently if one were to come up in future classes. I'm sure that those insecurities about my teaching authority might have gotten the better of me. Instead of giving Luke an appropriate amount of attention, and then washing my hands of him, putting the burden of responsibility for his education on his shoulders, I made it a project to get through to a student who was determined to resist me and get by with as little work as he could. The personal edge to our conflict (for example, his statement that I wasn't qualified to judge his writing, or the tougher comments I made on his papers) was clearly a complete waste of time on both sides. I think it's one of our main duties as teachers to maximize the potential that we discern in our students, and so it seems a bit tragic to let a promising, talented student schlep through my class. But at the same time, I might have used the time and energy that my dealings with Luke depleted on my other students. Instead of trying to transform Luke from an underachiever into a budding intellectual, I might have focused on transforming a less promising, marginal writer into a good one.

Postscript

When I originally composed this essay, soon after the conflict with Luke in my first semester of teaching, my thinking about what to conclude from our history was muddled and unsatisfying, no doubt because I was asking myself the wrong set of questions, concerned primarily with settling the blame for the conflict securely on one side of the student/teacher dyad. Was the conflict "Luke's fault"? Was I faced with the impossible situation of trying to get through to a student who would resist anything I had to say, precisely because he addressed me as another in a long series of teachers who had failed to understand him and consequently weren't worth listening to? Or was it "my fault," a matter of my insecurities as a new teacher, a defensive reaction against a student who I felt was covertly trying to attack my authority? I am tempted, in the interest of a well-proportioned conclusion, to parcel out the responsibility for the conflict equally (that is, Luke and I were reacting to each other like matter and antimatter; we just rubbed each other the wrong way). This set of questions leads to two possible conclusions, both of them not particularly enlightening in what they suggest as remedies for future relations with students like Luke. Either it was a matter of bad luck, stuck as I was with an "unreachable" student in my first writing class, in which case I can do little except hope that by the vicissitudes of karma or fate, I will be spared such a student in the future. Or conversely, I'm simply incapable of suppressing my frustration with students who address me like Luke did, in which case we arrive at the same inadequate solution, crossing our fingers and hoping that no new Lukes present themselves.

Since that first semester of teaching, I have not in fact had a relationship with a student anywhere near as frustrating and raw as this one. The lesson to draw from this is not that Luke was exceptionally unreachable (that I have lucked out in being spared another Luke), but rather that I have perhaps unconsciously settled into my role as teacher, learned to be comfortable with my authority or presence as a teacher, to the point where that defensive reaction against a perceived threat to my authority does not engage itself automatically. This conclusion is not much more satisfying than the last one, since it invokes nothing concrete in terms of what I've learned to *do* in the classroom. Essentially, it suggests a sort of "sink or swim" approach to learning how to teach: the first semester of teaching is necessarily frustrating and anxiety-provoking, but one can count on it getting better in the future (just as when learning to drive, one is unavoidably a bit anxious the first time one tries to parallel park on a busy street, but by doing it again and again, the anxiety eventually evaporates). As crude as this analogy is, I'm convinced that it's close to the truth; the conflict with Luke couldn't have erupted unless I was prepared to perceive every encounter with him as the latest battle in a never-ending war. This is not to suggest that Luke was a difficult student only in my imagination, a sort of projection of my insecurities, but rather that I was particularly vulnerable to the difficulties that Luke presented because of my obsession with questions like, Are they buying it? Am I a complete fraud as a writing teacher? Thus, while I cannot propose a checklist of suggestions for dealing with students like Luke, I can urge one to at least be conscious of this insecurity effect, and refrain from applying too much energy to "solving" problems that are elements of a *necessarily* frustrating and anxiety-producing experience, but, one hopes, a rewarding one as well.

15

Serving Byron

Case Study of an Obnoxious Student

Kuhio Walters

Preface

Before this semester, I spent two years teaching basic writing at a large public college in California's central valley (CSU-Fresno), and I carried many of the activities and theories from my teaching there into my classroom in Durham, New Hampshire. But things are very different here. For instance, only twice in California did I have white female students in my classroom, and all my students were from middle- to lower-class backgrounds. This semester, I had twenty middle- to upper-class white female students. Most of my students in California didn't really know what a private school was; many of my students here attended private middle schools and/or high schools. Most of my students in California lived off-campus, some of them in outlying farm towns; all my students here live on-campus. In the early portion of any given semester, my students in California rarely, if ever, questioned my pedagogical choices; this semester, students readily voiced their expectations of the class, and they were almost immediately happy to tell me if I wavered from those expectations.

In part, my study of Byron is an attempt to understand these different pedagogical challenges. But to clarify, I don't plan on resolving the differences between the two student populations, which is of course impossible; this is, for me, a matter of reevaluating how and why I teach. Here is something I wrote earlier in the semester:

> A Freirian sense of justice has always underscored my attitude toward students, but how does "a materialist rhetoric" [to borrow Alan France's borrowed term] of oppression and resistance square up with a student population that is *of* the ruling class? For the first time, I'm afraid of forcing a decontextualized political agenda onto my class. How "just" is it to assume I can simply transfer my pedagogy from one social-political-historical context onto any other context?

> I'm beginning to think it's impractical to spend time teaching privileged students that academic success has traditionally been reserved for privileged students. But even as I write these words, I realize I'm not willing to abandon my political convictions. What responsible person is, anyway?

This journal entry reveals the anxiety of a new teacher with limited exposure to different student communities. An important lesson I have learned since then is that the students here at UNH, while relatively homogenous in terms of class and ethnicity, do not have an innate "key" to academic success, and that there are conflicts in the classroom here that demand just as much ethnographic insight and compassion as any other classroom.

The larger agenda of this case study, then, is to affirm that, first and foremost, writing teachers must negotiate the unique learning needs of individual students. Ironically, this lesson for me has proven clearest in hindsight. The particulars of my experiences with Byron were most meaningful after the semester ended, as I read over everything he had written, jotted down recollections of his behavior in class, and explored patterns, connections, and interesting possibilities for interpretation. So in another sense, this case study—though Byron was for all practical purposes a successful student, garnishing an A for the course—is an account of failure on my part. As I will explain, I missed a significant teaching opportunity to help this student and the class as a whole better understand what it means to be "college material"; thus it's also a story of my development as a new teacher in a new environment.

Byron Goes to College

Byron is tall, wide, boisterous, arrogant, extremely bright—and the epitome of a "privileged" student. He is one of those students that, as Patricia Sullivan notes, comes "strutting into class, staking out their space and birthright" (Sullivan 1998, 250). This stereotype was reinforced when I got the class' first reading responses back. The first two readings I assigned were Lincoln Steffens' "I Go to College" and Malcolm X's "A Homemade Education." Both are autobiographical accounts dealing with higher education—Steffens' from the perspective of a wealthy, somewhat malcontented young white man, X's from the perspective of a counterhegemonic black man harboring deep resentment against the white establishment. As a whole, the class did not respond to this set of essays as I had expected—blatant naïveté on my part, now that I think about it. My experience with these essays had been with students that rallied behind X, but that had been in largely nonwhite classrooms. Here, Byron led the class with his criticism that "modern ethics have no place in history":

> Hundreds of years ago, people [...] saw every nation, every religion as an enemy, a competitor for ultimate superiority. [...][Throughout history,] it was not merely a question of whites against non-whites. Blacks fought Arabs. Arabs fought whites. Blacks fought blacks. Whites fought whites. Mongol

fought Chinese. This has always been the case and always will be. The English
in India were not racist in the sense that Malcolm X wishes us to believe. In
truth, they were more nationalist, seeking to expand their own empire and if
that was at the expense of someone else, so be it.

"In truth," Byron argues, there is a distinction between belligerent nationalism and racism. Racism is something everybody does; nationalism is something "the winners" do. This, of course, is expected ideology from a self-
professed "pro–capital punishment, anti–gun control," neoconservative. Like
many young, jingoistic xenophobes, his ideas take on the nebulous mix of
"Firing Line" propaganda and sophism; he is always pulled between uphold-
ing neoconservative ideals and tossing ideals out the window for the sake of
individualism—individualism being, in his view, the opposite of social deter-
minism and synonymous with superior intelligence. But this "inconsistency,"
of course, is not inconsistent at all. By adopting an "objective" stance toward
argumentation, by assuming that right and wrong is merely a matter of whose
rhetoric "wins" in the end, he actually avoids the uncomfortable discussion
of his own subjective and thus unstable foundations. He works very hard at
destabilizing truth so that he is always right, so that he can propose a "common
sense" which, coincidentally, is his own sense.

But interwoven with this theoretical instability is a quality to Byron's writing that suggests he does learn, or at least he's not an impenetrable zealot. He
wrote, for example, that revision could be

> difficult, and like all difficult things, it's good to ask someone else for help.
> After all, you are writing this for someone else to read it, so you might as
> well get someone else's opinion. You have to make sure to find someone with
> no advance knowledge of your assignment however, otherwise they may be
> biased by someone else's work. In any case, have them tell you everything they
> think is wrong with it. Then you tell them that they are wrong and you don't
> have to listen to any of their advice anyway. Then when they aren't looking,
> go back and make the changes they suggested. At least that's how I tend
> to do it.

This is a rich passage (and believe me, he's got a million of 'em). What strikes
me about it is its labyrinth of motives: he uses the assignment to display his
humor, which subverts his own (very real) cynicism toward the social nature
of writing—thus fulfilling the requirements of the assignment, yet subverting
the assignment; thus mocking me, yet pandering to me—all at the same time.
I doubt William F. Buckley is so clever.

Despite his love of his own "common sense," Byron shows a willingness
to laugh at himself (though more often at others). It was hard for me to con-
ceptualize at first, but I came to appreciate that he did indeed take writing
seriously, even though he constantly criticized the social dimension of writing,
the classroom's dynamics, and my pedagogy in general. He felt it important

to do what was required of him in class, to be officially validated, as well as continually reassert himself as an autonomous individual. This understanding of Byron as someone who expresses himself through humor—in various often caustic forms—explains why I so frequently cringe and laugh when reading even his most vile ramblings. Take this passage . . . please:

> Most of the kids in my [high school] classes were liberals and I had numerous encounters where I was lambasted for being pro–capital punishment, anti–gun control, and having common sense which liberals seem to lack. But then I came to college. People are even worse here.

Byron and Women

In a broader sense, his complex comedic performances suggest that his approach to scholarship is aggressive, full of challenging and questioning and self-defending, which is similar to his approach to world politics. Early in the semester, this played out in our classroom dynamics, considering the fact that in a room filled with women, Byron's voice was usually the most frequent, the loudest, and the most derisive. At times, his view on some of the women in our class bordered on misogyny. He labeled a group of women, who sat across the room from him, and with whom he continually bickered, "bitchy people" (the other bitchy people being liberals, in general). He stopped short of calling them bitches, probably because he was aware of my presence. Even with the women in his group (the other men in the class would have nothing to do with him), he was abrasive, often shunting productive small group work—though his interaction with them *he* considered friendly. I know for a fact that the women in his group did not always feel likewise. As I mentioned at the beginning of this essay, I started my work at UNH viewing my class as a more or less homogenous front—all white, all middle- to upper-class, all fluent in English. Any relationship with a new student population must begin, I suppose, from such a reduced perception. But it was not far into the semester before I realized there was more complexity here than I knew what to do with. What were my responsibilities to the women of the class? To each student? To Byron? To my own sense of social integrity?

For better or worse, here is how I handled the situation at the beginning of the semester. I would consider his views, which were usually well thought out, nodding my head all the while, and ask if anybody else had something to add. This seems a pragmatic enough course of action. But this was actually problematic because, I surmise, there was something about a big, noisy man aggressively blurting things out that turned some students away from entering the discussion. Michelle Payne has asked of her classroom, "in my efforts to be tolerant and egalitarian, do I have to value male values that I see as ultimately hurtful" (1994, 110)? I ask a similar question: in a class whose population is nearly 84 percent women, how do I respond to a student who deploys the discursive habits common to aggressive masculine discourse? Normally, there were only a few people who would willingly engage Byron's arguments (oddly enough, Byron's "bitchy people"), meaning I was often left with the brunt of the silence when he finished talking. Wondering how the other students in class were dealing with the situation, I handed out a class evaluation survey just before midterms, and there were, not surprisingly, numerous complaints about Byron's "corner."

Eighteen students commented on Byron's behavior in class, or on the behavior of the group of students he sat near (of which he was the dominant voice); but only one of my male students mentioned a problem with rudeness in the class: Byron. He wrote that the "difference between a good bitch and a bad bitch is the difference between Maddy and Josie. Maddy [one of the two students who sat next to Byron] admits she is a bitch and enjoys it, whereas Josie and Mary [two of the "bitchy people"] act nice then make snide remarks in scathing tones."

I will immediately qualify this by saying that Maddy *did* sometimes call herself a bitch; this isn't to justify Byron's sexism, but to note that his mention of Maddy was for him an act of camaraderie. (Unfortunately, I think Maddy would agree.) Calling Mary a bitch, however, was blatant sexism. The behavior Mary and Josie exhibited in class—rolling their eyes, mumbling snide remarks, snickering at Byron's comments—was effective because it turned his masculinist discourse on its head; they patronized his attempts at public performance, his main means of harvesting self-validation. This rhetorical castration was maddening for him, for he thought they were merely incapable of sustaining a "real" argument, and yet they succeeded in eventually silencing him. By the time midterm portfolios had been returned to the students, Byron was beginning to speak less and less in class. Admittedly, I was also to blame. Here is part of the handout that I gave them in response to their concerns in the class evaluations:

> *Complaints about complaining*: I will always allow people some space to vent concerns. In regards to rudeness and "over talkativeness," I think other students need to pick up the ball and structure the class the way they see fit. That means if you are bothered with somebody talking too much, or being rude, you need to speak up, or ask peers—who you know will speak up—to help you. This isn't an invitation to aggressiveness in class; it's an attempt to get you guys to take accountability for the classroom environment, to see that how the class runs is related to what you guys do—or don't do. Still, I will watch the clock and try to keep students from sucking up the class with dribble that's intended to consume time.

Rather suddenly, Byron's primary tool for expression was dissolving, both because of other students who were tired of his natural tendency to talk a lot, and by me, in that I explicitly encouraged other students to take a more active role in constructing their own ideal classroom environment—which, of course, was in response to him.

Meeting Byron

My discussion of Byron so far may be misleading. He was genuinely funny, took his writing seriously, and though he wouldn't say this openly, he really wanted to please me. There was something warmly human and smart about his comedic performances. From my description of him so far, you can image how pleased I was to receive this gem:

> I like to entertain, to make people laugh, or just perform for an audience. [...]
> Writing gives me another way to entertain. There is something about seeing
> your audience smile or laugh at a joke, or tap their fingers to the music. [...]
> As a writer, musician, or performer, there is something deep down that makes
> you feel good when you give something to those who are willing to take the
> time and effort to see you or your work. And frankly, I have yet to find a
> feeling in the world better than that.

I found this sincerity refreshingly uncharacteristic of him, for he is maudlin without a hint of self-deprecation. This is an explicit attempt on his part to explain (or more likely, justify) his usual flippancy, which suggests to me that he is attentive to the effect of his "antics" on a live audience, that his usual behavior is not merely an inability to apply academic conventions but rather a systematic application of his unique "voice." Even when I responded as I did to the class evaluations, it was not in resentment toward Byron; I was equally or perhaps more annoyed at Mary and Josie, since as a rule they were more into bugging him than they were into class discussion. Essentially, though he posed unique difficulties for how I ran my class, I wanted to like and be liked by Byron.

But I am not sure if we ever "connected" in anything more than a tense teacher/student relationship. Sometimes with students I can form bonds that move easily in and out of the classroom. I just cannot tell if this was the case with Byron. Coming home late one night, as I was crossing the street to get to my apartment complex, I heard the pounding of feet on pavement and somebody yelling my name. Byron came puffing out of the darkness, slowing casually to a walk by my side. We crossed the street together. Perhaps an opportunity, I thought, to crack this enigmatic nut. "Christ," I said to him, "you sound like a buffalo charging." "Buffalo?" he said. "I like to think I'm more of a bison. Buffalo is the term for a domesticated version of the bison, I think." (He was partly right. The name "buffalo" is restricted to African and Asian cattle that are of the bison family. The North American bison are much more temperamental. I looked it up.) We bantered for at least a half an hour, something we never really had the chance to do before or after class, or even in conference, since he was usually urgent to leave as soon as he got there. We stood under a street lamp. He talked a mile a minute, and, following his lead, I had to interrupt, raise my voice, and push ideas out in quick bursts just to get a word in edgewise. It was good fun, even though he talked 80 percent of the time. He had an arsenal of pre-scripted conservative arguments, deep rhetorical grooves that he could recite like a fervent priest—and I, a similar phalanx of Marxist quips. By the time we reached the base of my steps, we had even germinated the seed that would eventually become the topic for his research essay, the finest essay produced all semester. I was so involved that I stood out there for another hour, talking (listening).

We began walking again, and ended up beneath a street lamp on the other side of the complex. I asked him what he thought of the class, and he told me he thought I was too lax and needed to take more control. I was listening intently, having heard other students offer this same criticism. How quickly we can become insecure about things close to us: were my attempts at "leveling the playing field" backfiring, was our "alternative" classroom experience not nurturing them in the way I had wanted, was I doing more harm than good? I decided to be as honest and clear as possible. I laid out my pedagogical reasons for allowing class discussion to "do its thing," emphasizing to Byron, whether he liked it or not, the importance of students wielding some authority over their own classroom community. My argument was that it is healthy for students to use large group discussions to think aloud, that the teacher needs to be as small an influence in that process as possible, and that students must learn to take control of their own learning experience. His argument was that if I relinquished control, instead of the classroom community picking up the reins, one student would naturally take control—since, as he was learning in ROTC, the most effective workplace is one in which a single leader delegates tasks to a supportive rank and file. He offered himself as an example, telling of his experience in an ROTC exercise where he and a group of other prospective Air Force officers were placed in a confined space together, ordered to do a job, but not assigned with any specific chain of command. He was the one—and I totally believe this—who stepped forward into the role of leadership, and with a tone of, *listen, this is just common sense, let's do this,* he instructed the other men on how best to do what needed to be done. In other words, as far as he is concerned, if I were to lead efficiently, the students would be able to produce efficiently whatever it was that needed to be done. That is, he did not respect me because he felt I was incapable of gaining the respect of the class. Not only could Byron and I never really build a friendship because of my "flimsy liberalness" in the classroom, but our teacher/student relationship was, in his eyes, merely a ruse that must be maintained until the end of the semester. At most, I was a sounding board off of which he could bounce his repertoire of ultraconservative propaganda.

Reading Byron

In *The Interpretation of Cultures*, Clifford Geertz uses the analogy of winking to explain think description. If, for example, a student winks at you during your lecture, how should you interpret it? It might simply be a neurological hiccup, a sequence of physiological factors that results in the convulsing of facial muscles around the right eye. In that case it would make cultural sense to ignore it. But say it is a conspiratorial wink—the student has recognized something you said as witty; or perhaps, even more covert, he is flirting. Each different wink is a highly encoded cultural gesture with specific responses, and it is one of those acts in our culture that *must* be correctly interpreted, since the consequences for a flirtatious wink are very different from those for a nervous twitch. Furthermore, a conspiratorial wink is different than an imitation of a conspiratorial wink—for example if another student saw the first student winking at you, and was parodying the wink for other students out in the hall. And this wink is different than one that is done as a burlesque of the student in the hall, and is different than one rehearsed at home in front of a mirror. It is between a "think description" of what the rehearser of the burlesque fake wink is doing, and a "think description" of what he is doing, that Geertz says the "object of ethnography" lies:

> a stratified hierarchy of meaningful structures in terms of which twitches, winks, fake-winks, parodies, rehearsals of parodies are produced, perceived, and interpreted, and without which they would not [. . .] in fact exist, no matter what anyone did or didn't do with his eyelids. (1973, 7)

My reading of Byron is an attempt to emulate this method of investigation. At the beginning of the semester, I saw the equivalent of a twitch—indistinguishable from a conspiratorial, parodic, or burlesqued wink—in what Byron did. But my involvement with him taught me things about who he is and where he comes from, and as I begin to identify the "hierarchy of meaningful structures" from which he constructs his various selves, his idiosyncratic behavior in class and in his writing are beginning to make (some) sense to me.

For example, consider the militarized model of the classroom he presented to me that night in the apartment complex: students, if they're going to follow orders properly as well as eventually take on a leadership role, must be given explicit instructions in their duties. The teacher drives the course, making authoritative decisions and retaining the respect of the workforce so that they willingly do the work asked of them. This pedagogical metaphor illuminates the cultural values, assumptions, and biases with which Byron most closely associates: a single authority figure delegating explicitly defined behaviors to devoted workers, which is an ideal situation for the student who believes that with hard work, anybody can make it—if you don't make it, it is because you are lazy and/or not intelligent, and historically rooted oppression has nothing to do with it. But he also displays a fiercely individual "voice" in his writing, which doesn't readily mesh with the militarized classroom or with neoconservatism. He writes that:

> the most important thing I learned [in this class] was this: Listen to every one else's advice, but in the end, write what you want to write. [. . .] If someone says your style is wrong or inappropriate, tell them to (and you can quote me on this one) "Shove it." Writing should be clear and communicate your ideas, but you should do it on your terms, not someone else's.

He is always in conflict, realizing writing exists on a social level but resistant to the idea that he is not always in absolute control over how his meaning gets made. Writing is a site for rebellion, in the Rush Limbaugh sense of the word, and so he must constantly subvert academic purposes for writing, even as he meets their requirements.

At the beginning of this essay I related the uncertainty with which I first entered my classroom here at UNH. Not only did I have to change my pedagogy— like making sure all readings were relevant only for English as a first language students—I also had to change how I viewed my social agenda. Other than "raising student consciousness," I no longer felt the sense of urgency to discuss, for example, the exploitation of farm labor, or the stark lack of educational opportunities for Hmong girls. And with this, I wondered if there is even a place at UNH for non–literacy-oriented social agendas in composition. But this is what I am thinking at the moment: all teachers have a responsibility to work toward understanding their particular student body's "hierarchy of meaningful structures," through which we might better understand what it is about their environment that students most need to understand. For Byron, and for the other students in his class, what I should have done was spent some time discussing gendered discourses, and racisms and jingoism; but more importantly, I should have emphasized the social aspects of writing and the need for peer collaboration, and as Pat Sullivan suggests, offered "up the elite to the masses" (1998, 249), allowing Byron to learn from the influence of his peers, rather than passively fretting over how he was going to help or hinder my notion of social integrity.

16

"I'm Just Basic"

Reading Resistant Writers Within a Discourse of Resistance

Megan Fulwiler

"I believe, that because I know what I want to do, it makes it easier for me to sit back and laugh at the rest of the world. I guess you could say that I have a kind of security blanket or maybe a lawn chair, I don't know. I was never good with metaphors."—Jeff

RESIST—1. to strive or work against; oppose actively. 2. to remain firm against the action or effect of; withstand. 3. to keep from giving in to or enjoying.

My high school English teacher, Mrs. Schermer, made a deal with me about writing. The deal was that I could write the way I wanted to half the time, but I had to write her way the other half of the time—which was the five-paragraph theme. I knew what she wanted and I understood the "deal," but I continued to subvert and resist her assignments. I wrote what I wanted to and then tacked on a five-paragraph theme at the end. Sometimes I drew explicit attention to the limiting structure by writing "Oh yes, now I have to write a five-paragraph theme." I acknowledged her assignment but continued my own deliberate "misreading" of it. Now that I'm teaching college composition, it's time for payback. And Jeff is my payback.

In our first conference of the semester, I asked Jeff about the significant moments, memories, and images that he might write about for his Self Study. It was the first writing assignment in freshman composition, and I asked students to create a collage of meaningful "snapshots" from their lives that shaped who they were today. He sat across from me shrugging, too tall for the small desk chair, and said, "I don't know, I'm just basic." There was, he repeatedly stressed, nothing "different" about him. My attempts to question his third draft ("You really don't mention your Dad at all, do you want to? Is there something more for you to explore in this incident on page 2?") left him feeling resistant, and me feeling frustrated. My problem was that I didn't see any evidence of thoughtful revision, reflection, or introspection in his multiple drafts. His problem was the assignment of personal writing.

He wrote to me in the midterm portfolio reflection letter:

> I realize that you wanted me to get more personal in my writing, but that is as personal as I will get. I believe that you shouldn't share your most personal beliefs and thoughts to someone unless you have very strong feelings for them and trust them unconditionally. So you won't be seeing anything more personal than that freewrite I mentioned.

Three things came to mind when I read this letter: 1) I wanted to make a distinction between "personal" writing and "private" writing, 2) that Jeff had a clear sense of what I "wanted" but was not going to "give" it to me, and 3) he *had* these personal feelings, but that as a teacher I did not fit the criteria for sharing. On many levels I understand and respect this response. On another level—the level that has been stumped more than once in a conference with him—I felt that his resistance merited a lower grade. After all, he did not do the assignment. I asked for self-examination and reflection. I got a montage of party scenes and a catalogue of family members. I've thought about Jeff a lot (it's hard not to), and I've become interested in the ways that "resistance" as discourse, pedagogy, and practice gets played out in the writing classroom. I began to wonder about the situation of a resistant writer who opposes both a resistant pedagogy and a teacher who has always considered herself a resistant reader.

I am a resistant reader. Judith Fetterley first coined the term in the context of feminist literary criticism with her book *The Resisting Reader*. This approach to reading looks for gaps, absences, and silences within a text; Mike Bal has called it reading for "counter coherence." I see a close alignment between this act of literary criticism and Lad Tobin's phrase "misreading." In reading most student texts, argues Tobin, "we use our skill, experience and imagination to read (*or misread*) these student texts in productive ways; that is, we have learned to listen to what is not yet being said and to read through the text for meaning, nuance, tension, potential" (1996, 58:163, emphasis mine). In reading and responding to male personal narratives, Tobin argues that we need to read for these same kinds of narrative gaps and silences—even with student papers that we question.

I read Tobin around the same time that I read Jeff's Self Study. And I read for these gaps, absences, and discontinuities in Jeff's writing. But Jeff's brand of resistance *resisted* this kind of reading because he opposed the writing assignment itself. Jeff's opening paragraph of his final Self Study sets up his ambivalence about the assignment:

> Who is Jeff Miller? Is he some sort of enigma, a mystery wrapped in a puzzle? Well now I don't know about all that, but I believe Popeye said it best when he said, "I am what I am" and that's how I feel about myself as well. I don't believe that I'm that complicated of a person. It's hard for me to describe myself due to my lack of eccentricities. However, if I had to give a summary of my personality I guess I'd use words like sense of humor, sarcastic, cynical, honorable, laid back, and hardworking. I'm more a lover than a fighter, more rock and roll than country, and all the rest just kind of falls into place. All and all I'd say I'm a pretty decent guy.

Reading this now, I notice how he has "misread" my assignment—a Self Study has been reduced to a "summary." I can see the resistance to my notions of multiplicity and contradictions when he says that he doesn't believe that he's "that complicated of a person." But I also smile when he writes that he's "more rock and roll than country." As a reader, I feel his reluctance and anxiety; as a writing teacher I want him to examine that further. All my attempts at reading for gaps, contradictions, or discontinuities were an utter failure because he didn't see any in his writing, in his "self," or in his life. Later in his piece, he writes, "So you can see I'm not a very hard person to understand. As a matter of fact, I think I'm a lot like most people out there in the world, and by that I mean you won't be seeing me on Jerry Springer any time soon." Jeff's sense of "self" and personal identity is grounded in the firm (indeed, unshakable) belief that he is like "most people out there" and therefore doesn't want to examine his own social, familial, and emotional makeup. He's confident in his future, his past, and seemingly his present. Jeff's stance as a writer raises important questions for me; is it my job as a writing teacher to ask students to critique and question their "position" in this world?

The first-year writing class is often positioned as a site of resistance. It is the ideal place—perhaps the most important place—to teach critical examinations of the multiple factors that inform one's "self," one's language, and one's culture. The writing class can be a place to resist and critique dominant discourses and social practices. Joseph Harris advocates teaching students to "write as critics of their culture" and advocates for "classrooms that do not simply reproduce the values of our universities and cultures but that also work to resist and question them" (1991, 58). The realm of the classroom, then, is constructed as a place where students can talk and *talk back to* the authorities of both texts and institutions.

Resistance and writing are continually tied closely to change, social justice, and intellectual pursuits. As editors C. Mark Hurlbert and Michael Blitz write in their introduction to *Composition and Resistance*, "Writing, itself, is a struggle in and *with* social order" (1991, 4, emphasis mine). The writing classroom, then, is constructed as a forum of resistance and struggle where students are invited to resist dominant discourses that perpetuate social inequity and oppression. And composition teachers themselves are called on to resist dominant and traditional modes of teaching, reading, and researching.

Positioning the composition classroom as a class of "resistance" creates a paradoxical situation for the teacher. We are authority figures who teach resistance to authority. The role of the composition teacher seems uniquely situated within the larger academic world of teaching—even within the smaller world of English departments. As James Berlin argues, "Our larger purpose is to encourage our students to resist and to negotiate these codes—these hegemonic discourses—in order to bring about more personally humane and socially equitable economic and political arrangements" (1991, 50). As writing teachers, we offer an alternative to traditional models of teaching, reading, and writing. The composition classroom fosters opportunities for interactive learning, a process approach, agency, and student ownership of their words. We "resist" traditional teaching that is teacher centered, lecture formatted, and that values memorization over active learning. "We can teach writing," claim Hurlbert and Blitz, "as the material out of which we not only (re)create ourselves and others, our understanding of culture, ethnicity, gender, sexuality, class, but also as the material with which we can resist those narratives when they do *not* accurately reflect our real life" (1991, 7).

Our position as teachers can be one of resistance, our pedagogy can become one of resistance, and our classroom can be claimed as a space for resistance. But I'm becoming wary of all this talk about resistance because I don't see either myself or Jeff reflected back in this conversation. Jeff's issue wasn't with his narrative at all—it was with my seeking to problematize that narrative. Within the rhetoric of resistance, there is little mention of the students who won't buy in, who won't "play the game," and who take a stance of "resistance." The more I read, the more I realize that my concerns about Jeff's writing were not that he refused to resist hegemony, but that he refused to move beyond the surface level of his own life.

As the semester progresses, I learn more about Jeff. He wants to become a cop, live in Seattle, and own a dog. Jeff is a constant presence in the classroom—in fact, he never misses a single class or conference. He completes each assignment, uses humor in interesting ways, and writes up one of the best interviews with an outside source. He chooses boxing as the topic for his final Researched Essay and it is informed, interesting, and considers historical and social angles. Not surprisingly, I don't agree with his position on boxing, but I'm trying to help him articulate it more clearly and to discover his own stance. Like my teacher Mrs. Schermer, I wish that I had been able to strike a "deal" with Jeff back in September, but perhaps, in our own way, we have.

17

"I Am an Excellent Writer"

One Composition Instructor's Puzzlement About Bullying and Plagiarism

Freda Hauser

As I near the end of my first semester of teaching freshman composition, I find that I have accumulated questions, which now lie in front of me like the pieces of a puzzle. I pick them up, one by one, and peer at the others before me, looking for a shape and pattern into which each might fit. I think maybe, if I could just visualize what the box top looks like, I would have a picture of the meeting place that is the classroom, a meeting place of conversation, of teaching, of a multitude of experiences.

As I search through them, two of the gaudier pieces stand out; they have those wavy edges that make them look like one piece when set side by side. Curiously enough, the wave forms a question mark. The two sides of the question are these: How do we deal with plagiarism? How do we deal with bullies?

We have probably all known the bully—let's call him Joe. I can remember the first time I met one. I was in kindergarten, and a little boy in my class used to wait behind the cars in the parking lot and throw stones at me as I walked by. "He's a bully," my teacher said.

Now teaching, I run into "Joe" again. He sits and whispers to his neighbors while I talk, darting looks of daring at me. I assign an essay by Dorothy Allison. When I introduce her as an activist on matters of class, feminism, and lesbian rights, Joe nudges his neighbor. Pointing at me, he whispers audibly, "I told you so!" His act seems calculated to target me as possible other, an other whom, in his eyes, may be named, with impunity, as shameful. Does he understand what boundaries are, where they lie? After all, there is no placement test for maturity. Do I confront him directly? How do I cope with the way that other students sitting near him seem to turn sour faces toward me every time I speak? I cannot, after all, silence him completely. Can I defuse him?

The first time I conference with Joe, he slouches into the room, baseball cap proudly hailing me from its slanted angle. Even his act of sitting feels aggressive to me, even before he folds his arms across his chest and plants his legs firmly astride the sides of the chair. "I," he announces, in a confident tone, "am an excellent writer."

Taken aback, I mutter something about being glad he is so confident, what an asset that will be to his writing, and listen as he tells me about his honors English class the year before in high school, his excellent grades, and his top prize for his final essay.

Joe refuses to rewrite papers. If it needed changing, he would have done so already. His "old" teacher (a man) had no problems with his work; in fact "that teacher" praised it. Then Joe fakes a reference, making up an article to fill the request for sources. He gives me a "rough draft" of a researched essay two weeks early. All the other students are working on their research; I have seen none of his. I am immediately suspicious. I read it and waver. The language reads like his in places; in other places it reads like an encyclopedia. We conference, and I ask questions. He slouches back in his chair, arms crossed over his shirt, and answers glibly.

I think about what I've seen my own children do, just barely paraphrasing, internalizing the encyclopedia's writing style, and blending a very few sources. I have raved in horrified tones and been told, "But Mom, this is how we're supposed to do it." I have seen my older son penalized for including original thinking in his essays because: "it wasn't the assignment." Is this what and how Joe has learned? Then how do I convince him there are alternatives?

And how do I judge where his intention lies? I can tell he's looking for an easy out. Maybe he got this from a fraternity brother, from a friend—most likely he wrote it in high school. All of these, according to the Freshman Composition Handbook, are kinds of plagiarism, making him subject to immediate failure. But I can't prove it, can I?

Why must this be so complicated? I ask myself. Why no simple answers? I try different responses, all based on concepts of "tough love" and active listening from an old Parent Effectiveness Training course. My work with Joe moves slowly. The puzzle pieces seem to melt in my hands like some Lewis Carroll dream—they become dense as liquid lead. And then I begin to realize the parts of *my* reactions that partially form the puzzle.

I speak with my father, who has taught for forty years, on the phone. He thinks I am making a mistake. Kick him out! This is his advice: that such students are like a virus, infecting the classroom with their venomous attitude. (He did not teach English and so feels free to use mixed metaphors.) I ask in my father's terms: how can we best set up limits in the classroom? I add in my own: and without participating in bullying? It would be so easy to act in a mean spirit right back. Even if I can contain my emotional reactions, how can I teach the student after I ask him to leave? Do I kick the bullies right out?

Because isn't the other point, the real point, that the student who is a bully is not learning, so far, because he is more engaged with the idea of holding the controls than with asking questions? Isn't this what being a bully is all about? And doesn't one of the rationales of plagiarism whisper that at least someone else must have had control of the information, since the person was published? And (I ask in a hushed voice) can you teach someone to *want* to ask questions? I wonder (and feel blasphemous): is he teachable? Are there students who, because of their socialization, are not teachable? Or, is it my identity that is the problem? I could have named this bully "Josephine," but the gender difference complicates the picture. I tell myself that he would probably listen more easily to a male teacher, especially one who is unmistakably (in his eyes) heterosexual. But would he? And does "real" learning come because someone who is in the shape that is coded "respectable" teaches you?

I think of my mother. I remember going home from kindergarten, furious at having had another day of dodging rocks, and being upset at my mother's response, which was to invite that earlier Joe over to play. He was really a coward, she said, all bullies are cowards, lonely too. I ask, in my mother's terms: what is the pain of not being seen through that mask? Who will see, really, how frightened you are? Who will notice that this is not your voice? Who cares? How lonely! And yet these fears feed the bullying.

Yes, these two questions link. It takes a kind of bullying swagger to plagiarize, to claim to someone else that the work of another is your own. In a way you challenge them to "see" you, to "name" you, pirate or thief. Perhaps you think you wear a disguise, which no one can penetrate. You are the clever one. But plagiarism also carries that dark shadow of the coward, the frightened one.

And I hold my own fears. I am afraid to ask these questions, afraid to be thought stupid, or resistant, or worst of all, bad at what I do. And these questions are complicated by so many factors, by being, for example, a feminist who does want to model strong—but not patriarchal—behavior. They are complicated by trying to come out of the closet as a lesbian—hoping I will be seen as neither a threatening monster nor hurt victim. Mostly they are complicated by working against a lifetime of fear—a fear initiated by bullying, perpetuated by the further fear of becoming that which I fight against.

There have been times, with almost every student I have ever taught, when it is as if I look into a mirror, forced to come to grips with certain possibilities of being. This moment, hovering along the borderland of the theft that is plagiarism and the cowardice that is bullying, turns those puzzle pieces into mirrors. I have no answers. I invite you, the reader, to look into those mirrors with me. What do you see?

18

Redefining Success

Kathleen Toomey Jabs

The Literacy Narrative. The name alone sounded sufficiently high-minded for me to want to assign one. I envisioned attending a future staff meeting, or even more grand, a composition conference, and saying with practiced nonchalance, "I've had such success with my students' literacy narratives." The other instructors would nod, hastily finish their cheese, and rush to speak, perhaps with jalapeño still in their teeth, about their own success stories. I imagined success a noble goal—it wasn't all about me (at least not totally); I was going to get to know my students, show them the power and joy in writing, and win a flock of converts. When I received the literacy narratives, I planned to analyze the class' backgrounds and abilities, compose psychological and grammatical profiles of the students, design individual exercises, hold conferences, get to know the students through their writing. I held hopes of students fondly reminiscing about their favorite books and authors (particularly literary fiction ones), perhaps complaining about a torturous senior research paper, but nevertheless admitting they looked forward to a class that allowed them the chance to write and rewrite and write again. (I am not hopelessly naïve; as a graduate student I read, write, and rewrite for a living.)

The first few papers were reassuring. I nodded, smiled, made comments in the margin. And then I read the fifth paper. Jason wrote: "I guess I will tell you strait [sic] out, I suck at writing. I always have, and I probably always will. I have no strengths. I only have weaknesses. I have no likes. I only have dislikes." I was struck by the plaintiveness of the voice, by the utter despair seemingly muffled in the words. Despite the opening, the whole essay was not morose; in fact, while I didn't exactly like the content, I found myself admiring the rhythm and balance of the words. The voice had a certain style.

Jason used profanity as well as humor throughout the essay, and I wondered if the word choice was for shock value or if it was meant as a test of my standards. Was I going to allow profanity? I hadn't considered that question. How about sexual innuendo? Another issue I hadn't considered. While I don't see myself as a prude, profanity and sexual innuendo in the first assignment of a freshman composition class were not what I expected. Was it a challenge? Was I supposed to ignore it? Encourage it? Request that it be changed?

Jason closed his essay (after another paragraph about how and why he disliked writing and had no hopes or achievements), with the following:

> I think I can imagine my first love . . . She was 5'10" and had long blond hair . . . Oops! Wrong first love. I don't recall having a love for writing. Ever. But I do remember being afraid of it. I've always had a fear of it. And I've always had this fear that what ever [sic] I write sounds and looks horrible.

My reactions to this paper were dichotomous. I wondered how I might probe Jason for details about why he had hated writing without sounding as if I was trying to psychoanalyze him (which I partially was). I also wondered if perhaps I was being overly sensitive to him, when he obviously wasn't to me.

We met in conference and I attempted to ask Jason questions that I thought might draw out and perhaps even cure his writing phobia: "Why do you hate writing? Can you recall a specific instance where writing might have become negative for you? Have you had any memorable experiences with English?" He merely sat in the chair and responded negatively to my queries. With the silence in the office, my own self-consciousness merely increased. I tried to reassure Jason that specific details were part of good writing, that he could strengthen his story and relate to his audience (his class peers) more if he provided examples for things. He blushed and remained silent, a continuing feature of our conferences. I tried to reassure him that his voice was unique and that his paper seemed insightful, even humorous, but I received no affirmation, no breakthrough, not even a nod. When he left I looked at my watch; it had only been ten minutes, but I estimated I had said "um like" seventy-two times.

One week into class and I was tempted to write Jason off. There were, after all, twenty-three other needy students, students with promise, at least half of whom seemed to want to be there. Jason was from Newmarket, ten minutes south of Durham on Route 108, and thus the graduate of a local high school that prided itself on its mule mascot. In a postconference uncharitable moment, I thought maybe a mule had kicked Jason and altered his brain or that he had acquired the mascot's characteristics by wearing too many school team shirts. Yet, that moment passed and it occurred to me that I was intrigued by Jason's defiance, his insistence that he "sucked" at writing, when, at least in my opinion, he did not. I decided he would be my success story. I would change his view of writing.

The next paper assignment was the personal narrative. We spent a week in class doing brainstorming and freewriting exercises in anticipation of the upcoming essay. As I walked around the classroom I noticed that Jason's notebook was often blank, that he seemed to stare straight ahead of him or merely down at his paper. He never volunteered to share anything and was quiet within his small groups. He caused no trouble, asked no questions. Yet, when I received his personal narrative during a "cold conference" of all things, I was shocked. He had not written one; what he had done was, in fact, nothing like what I had asked. He invented his narrative, created an event, a persona even, based on a scenario he said he observed in his dorm.

Jason's story began, "I was sitting at my computer one cold night, typing a paper much like this one but only different. *Really.* I heard voices out in the hallway, so I decided 'what the heck,' I might as well check out who was disturbing my genius train of thought." I was hooked. The voice promised humor and Jason carried through with that, claiming the paper he was writing would win him the Nobel Prize. Even the sarcasm seemed promising. Although it was somewhat negative humor, I could see Jason perhaps laughing at himself, the irony apparent both to reader and writer.

The humor was not as enjoyable, however, when I got to the bottom of the page. There, Jason proceeded to describe a girl at the end of the hall, "wearing small, tight shorts, and a tight shirt. God she looked delicious." I tried to keep an open mind, reminding myself that this was after all, personal writing—his person, not mine. I read on. Jason imagined a football player appraising the girl at the end of the hall and he (the imaginary Jason) confronting the football player and challenging him. In this dream/vision, Jason told the football player, "We all know what you are thinking: 'Damn she has some nice legs. Hmm I wonder what kind of panties she's wearing?'" The voice became somewhat confusing as Jason tried a complicated technique: he was trying to describe a conversation in his head and the imagined responses of the football player and then the girl.

At the beginning of the conference with Jason I was at a loss. While the paper was clearly not a personal narrative, it was an innovative attempt and it encompassed risk, something I had emphasized to the class. From Jason's literacy narrative, I knew how sensitive he was to criticism. I found myself trying to reassure him about the merit of the paper, the originality of the idea. Jason began to open up and to talk about what he was attempting to do and why. He was still vague, but he offered some insight: "I just wanted to try something different from the old personal experience, I did this, that, and the other thing. You know, I wanted to try something different."

I repeated my admiration for his humor and his willingness to try something different. During the conference his initial resistance seemed to ease a bit and I thought that we might have entered new ground. By the time we went over the problems in the narrative that made the flow difficult to follow, Jason seemed receptive to the changes and even offered his own ideas, saying, "I think I might have him saying that. And where it says like 'the average Joe,' I'm probably going to have to say that." His revised draft did indeed have the changes we discussed and it was much more coherent. I claimed a victory.

A few weeks later, we embarked on the research essay and I assigned one of Bruce Ballenger's exercises from *The Curious Researcher.* The students were supposed to "fast write" about their topics and engage in a dialogue with an imaginary person. I collected the responses and skimmed them, looking for effort. When I came to Jason's it did not look unusual, but as I focused in, I saw that what I had assumed to be freewriting was not. Instead Jason has written:

> My thinking hasn't changed. The only thinking I have done is about how much this research thing sucks. Now don't get me wrong I like researching but I hate all these dumb ass ex. that we have to do w/ it. They seemed pointless. I can understand the Works Cited thing and NB checks to see if we know how to do something. I can see that. I like that but we could be doing something more important and useful w/ our time.

I cringed. Such hostility. And he had handed it in. I admired Jason's bravery and willingness to tell the truth as he saw it as much as I was challenged by the remarks. There wasn't much comfort to be found, but I was glad that Jason at least was enjoying the researching. When the class reflected on differences and similarities between this research paper and past ones, Jason wrote, "This research paper was very different from all the other research papers. It wasn't (or didn't seem) boring and monotones [sic], it had a little spice to it. It also had an informal tone, like a fun kind of tone." And so it did, if you considered his tone funny, which I worked hard to do, because I didn't.

Unlike the humor in his other papers, the humor Jason used in his research paper seemed contrived, even forced. He was trying so hard to be funny that he wasn't. He opened his paper with a quote from Groucho Marx, "One morning I shot an elephant in my pajamas. How he got in my pajamas I'll never know." He then went on to write:

> You might ask yourself, what does this quote have to do with salt marshes? I will answer you with this: elephants in pajamas do not live in salt marshes. Give me a break I am trying to be original. Ok [sic], now back to the subject at hand. Where was I, oh yeah, I have not even started, so the best place to start would be at the beginning with a little bit of early human use.

I tried to see the opening as funny, but in conference I suggested to Jason that he might want to consider other beginnings, maybe to sharpen the humor or keep it more related to the project and voice he wanted to carry through the piece. He had an interesting personal anecdote on page three about his first encounter with a salt marsh, and I suggested that he might want to expand and open with that.

Needless to say, he didn't take my advice. He revised very little in the paper. I was tempted to assign him an F for Failure to Listen. I realized I was vested in my own recommendations. The paper, although somewhat boring, fulfilled the criteria of the assignment, and while Jason didn't offer any personal insights, he had used a variety of sources and organized the material. I put the essay away to grade later and tried not to think about all the "dumb-ass" exercises he thought I assigned.

Jason surprised me in the final questionnaire by writing that the research paper was the most enjoyable assignment for him. Yet a few sentences later, he undercut his pronouncement with the statement, "I don't know why I liked the assignment, maybe because I put down what I already knew down on paper. I didn't have to do any major research, maybe it was because I could sound smart for once in my life."

Sounding smart. No major research. Those words stung. But, I took to heart that he admitted he liked the assignment. The other words didn't seem an attempt to win sympathy or pity; they were just a reflection of the weakened self-esteem of a student whose confidence I had tried to bolster. Although I was bothered by Jason's critique of his own stories, I was even more troubled by his final reflective letter/essay. After sixteen weeks of process writing, Jason wrote, "I don't feel that my writing has improved thus far in freshman composition. My writing still sucks. . . . The only papers that come remotely close to what I like writing are personal experiences and when I can complain about something."

Despite my requests for personal experience papers, Jason never wrote one. His personal experience essay was a fictional narrative (although I suspect he is the one looking at the girl and thinking the football player's thoughts). And his research essay had very little connection to any personal interest or experience with salt marsh. The only personal insights into Jason came at the end of the semester as we were doing a series of culture surveys. After sharing a particularly foul comedian tape with the class, Jason wrote about it and exposed some of his insecurity. His reflection piece concluded with the sentence: "I don't know why I have to live in such a freaky generation, but it seems like there are going to be less and less [sic] 'normal' people by the time we reach the age of 30 or 40. Oh well, it gives me something to look at, and keeps live [sic] interesting."

Although he puts normal in quotes, it's clear that Jason sees himself as one of the last remaining vestiges of normalcy. He is besieged, surrounded, and he seems to have nowhere to ground himself. When he writes on an issue that makes him angry, his defensiveness is even more apparent—"What really pisses me off is when I play basketball at Newmarket with Newmarket kids. I hate them. They are cocky sons of bitches. It's okay to be cocky, but you have to have the proof to back it up." I would argue that Jason's humor, his sarcasm, and his use of profanity are not a reflection of his own cockiness, but rather of his own fear of being different, of being recognized for that, and of facing a world without clear boundaries.

How does a new instructor or even an experienced professor provide reassurance to someone that it's okay to be different, especially when the difference is stylistically not to his or her liking? This semester didn't give me an answer to that. I allowed Jason's profanity, his sexual innuendo, asked him questions in conferences, tried to encourage him to write about issues and things with personal meaning, but, like Jason, I saw no change from the beginning to end of the semester. I wish I could have reassured Jason, could have injected him with the self-confidence he seemed to lack, could have made him see that his writing did not "suck." But none of those things happened. He was not the success story I envisioned, and he actively stamped out any validation that my class made a difference in his writing or his life.

Yet, I do not consider Jason a write-off or a complete failure. Working with him challenged me, forced me to examine my own needs and to ask—do I really need validation? Is it not enough to know the subject has been covered, that I, as well as the students have taken risks? Is my own "self" dependent on the performance of my students' "selves"? Is the act of serving enough?

19

Girl Trouble

Amanda Glenn

I try to be nice to all my students, male or female. But when it comes to being the conductor of consequences for irresponsibility, the "nice" factor gets in the way.

On the first day of class, Heather told me that she had Lyme disease. My knowledge of the disease was minimal, but she told me that she might miss a class or two due to morning nausea. I told her that we'd work out the assignments or exercises she missed, and didn't worry about it further. Since she had waited to speak to me until everyone left the room, I had the impression that she was not a person who wanted her privacies revealed. She seemed reliable, responsible.

Weeks later, I had seen very little of Heather. Her papers were handed in, though late, and she missed every scheduled conference. I advised her to drop the course, but she refused. There is a tightening of gaze and a flicker behind the eyes when women have to say unpleasant things to each other. Heather gave me this as I told her how much work she had to make up in a week's time. She amiably responded that I hadn't made the assignment clear. I admit I flickered, too, and replied something generic, while wondering if she was right. Students who make you question your authority know what they're doing, and it is frustrating to butt heads with their logic. Had she been in class the day of the assignment, I later realized, Heather would not have been able to accuse me of being unclear.

I told her to stay in touch and to email me when she was absent: "It's your responsibility to keep on top of your work," I said, feeling the impotence of the words as they bounced off her turned back. Our relationship was quickly becoming clear: Heather had armored herself within a system that worked for her; doctors and health problems were her mechanism for working through every conversation with me. Her personal life took priority. I was not surprised by this; I am aware that my class is not the focal point of my students' lives. What made me uncomfortable was that Heather seemed to expect me to prioritize her personal life as well. Her life, her problems, took precedent over our class.

107

I was apparently supposed to understand that—and expect it. I had told the class to email me if they were going to be absent in order to get their missed assignments. When Heather did email me, it would simply be to say that she wasn't going to make it to class, telling me without remorse that she'd overslept or had an important test to study for. I was at a loss. Well, I had told her to keep in touch.

After an absence of a week or two, Heather showed up for the last twenty minutes of a class and waited to talk to me afterwards. This meeting was unlike our original discreet encounter; she stepped ahead of the five students waiting to speak with me, and announced in a ringing voice that she was sorry she'd missed so much class, but she now had a problem with eating disorders and was spending a lot of time with her doctor. My reaction was hardly authoritative; I was no more well prepared for this diatribe than were her fellow students, who assumed various poses of deafness. I eyed her, glanced skeptically at the (again late) paper she'd handed me, and mumbled, "That's okay."

In the weeks before I undertook teaching English 401, I'd been warned about problem students: boys. Big tall half-men who would physically intimidate me and sneer at my assignments. No one had mentioned problem girls. I thought at first that these students were only a problem on a female-to-female basis, a sure explanation for the silence surrounding this topic. But after tentatively mentioning Heather's situation to my peers, I found that men in the department had had confrontations with female students as well. Why, then, if this had happened before, did no one talk about it? Is it easier to dismiss the resistance of a female student as a character flaw—a personal difficulty rather than an academic one?

To generalize, male students seem to have a clearer sense of black and white—their papers need work, but I still like them personally, and even if I don't still like them, I'm just their teacher. Female students connect their academic assessments much more closely with the personal. It is more difficult to divorce the two, perhaps because a conference between two females can seem like a social situation. Maybe my male students feel that the gender difference creates greater distance between us.

The situation with Heather was one that I was unprepared to handle, one that no one else, at first, seemed to have. I assumed that it was my fault. It must have been me and my new-teacher dilemma of developing a good teacher-student relationship. I must, I thought, have done it wrong with Heather. And, at least to a certain extent, I did. Because here's the bottom line: why didn't I tell Heather exactly what I required of her at that moment? I wanted to be nice. And I didn't just want to be nice to her; I was caught off-guard in front of several students: definitely the wrong time to subject all present to a harangue on responsibility.

Adding to the situation was the difference in the way male and female instructors relate to students. I felt a greater need to be sympathetic than my male colleagues, one of whom said heartlessly, "Fail her." I felt guilty over

Heather's failing grade, and I knew that when I told her of her failure it would be with more apologetic tone than was necessary. Instead of telling her what work was due, perhaps I should have told her specifically that she would fail if work were not turned in on time. Perhaps I shouldn't have given her an extension on that solitary occasion when she came to my office looking genuinely ill. Perhaps by not listing for Heather every possible way she could fail the course, I was at fault.

Women colleagues have mentioned the irritation of facing harder arbitration with their male students than their male colleagues. I feel the reverse can be true as well. I should be sympathetic, Heather implies, because I've introduced myself to the class that way, or perhaps more significantly, because we're both girls. Her original mention of her disease had been brief and professional. Since then, the excuses became more involved and personal: roommate complaints, doctor stories, parental worry. I was suddenly drawn into the midst of my student's life, with more knowledge of her daily strife than I wanted or felt I should have. And I may have been too sympathetic to her at first, encouraging this behavior with what I thought was patience with her increasingly complex problems.

Mixed with the guilt, though, was doubt through irritation. The flexibility tests through which my grading policy had been run made me crabby. Was an F reasonable, I wondered, or simply retaliation? After all, I was getting tired of the intricate games that were being played. If I had any doubt about Heather's just desserts grade-wise, wouldn't it just be easier to fail her and get the whole difficulty behind me?

The paper Heather handed me the day of her newest announcement was about a time she was raped. It was disorganized and full of cliché; but how can such a paper not be? I couldn't give Heather the low grade her paper deserved without first speaking with her, and part of me objected to grading the paper at all; there are schools of thought that argue both in favor of and against the use of such highly personal material in 401. Before actually entering my classroom, I had thought myself to be a member of the "write it all down" school. It would be good, I thought, for my students to feel that they could write whatever they wanted; it would make their writing more personal and original. Then I got Heather's rape paper. There was no way I could grade such a thing. I certainly didn't want to ask her to develop the paper's undeveloped details, or tell her that her word choices weren't convincing. But I'd said that the class could write about anything. How could I say, "Well—anything but that"?

The main problem with the paper, though, was Heather's refusal to come to conference. I couldn't comment on the paper if she was not there to listen. She had thrown a shocker paper at me and had disappeared like a magician in a conjured puff of smoke. I had been successfully thrown off her trail.

Despite the doubt, however, there was no conceivable way that Heather could pass the class given all that she'd missed. I steeled myself and prepared to tell her the news, rather than let her be "surprised" when grades came out. But she beat me to it. An email notifying me that she was leaving school brought a quick end to my resolve, as well as a disappointing dénouement for the entire exchange.

So now I don't know how it would have ended. I don't know if I would have been firm and unyielding, denying eleventh-hour requests to make up work, or listened unfeelingly to more medical reports. I don't know if Heather would have tried for a last-ditch sympathy plea.

I still try to be nice to all my students. But whatever suppositions they may have regarding their priorities in my class are their responsibility to sort out, and for most freshmen this is an unprecedented freedom. I don't have to make their decisions to come to class; I just grade them once their choices are made.

References

Berlin, James A. 1991. "Composition and Cultural Studies." In *Composition and Resistance*, edited by C. Mark Hurlbert and Michael Blitz. Portsmouth, NH: Boynton/Cook.

Dethier, Brock. 1999. *The Composition Instructor's Survival Guide.* Portsmouth, NH: Boynton/Cook.

Geertz, Clifford. 1973. *The Interpretation of Cultures.* New York: Basic Books.

Harris, Joseph, and Jay Rosen. 1991. "Teaching Writing and Cultural Criticism." In *Composition & Resistance*, edited by C. Mark Hurlbert and Michael Blitz. Portsmouth, NH: Boynton/Cook.

hooks, bell. 1994. *Teaching to Transgress: Education as the Practice of Freedom.* New York: Routledge.

Hurlbert, C. Mark, and Michael Blitz, eds. 1991. "Resisting Composure." *Composition and Resistance.* Portsmouth: Boynton/Cook.

Murray, Donald. 1999. *Write to Learn.* Fort Worth, TX: Harcourt Brace.

Newkirk, Thomas. 1997. *The Performance of Self in Student Writing.* Portsmouth: Boynton/Cook.

Payne, Michelle. 1994. "Rend(er)ing Women's Authority in the Writing Classroom." In *Taking Stock: The Writing Process Movement in the 90s*, edited by Lad Tobin and Thomas Newkirk. Portsmouth: Boynton/Cook.

Perl, Sondra, and Nancy Wilson. 1986. *Through Teachers' Eyes: Portraits of Writing Teachers at Work.* Portsmouth, NH: Heinemann.

Sullivan, Patricia. 1998. "Passing: A Family Dissemblance." In *Coming to Class: Pedagogy and the Social Class of Teachers*, edited by Alan Shepard, John McMillan, and Gary Tate. Portsmouth, NH: Boynton/Cook.

Tobin, Lad. 1996. "Car Wrecks, Baseball Caps, and Man-to-Man Defense: The Personal Narrative of Adolescent Males." *College English* 58: 158–75.